Abstracts

of the

BALTIMORE COUNTY

◆ M ◆ A ◆ R ◆ Y ◆ L ◆ A ◆ N ◆ D ◆

LAND COMMISSIONS

1727-1762

Baltimore County Genealogical Society

HERITAGE BOOKS
2015

HERITAGE BOOKS

AN IMPRINT OF HERITAGE BOOKS, INC.

Books, CDs, and more—Worldwide

For our listing of thousands of titles see our website
at
www.HeritageBooks.com

Published 2015 by
HERITAGE BOOKS, INC.
Publishing Division
5810 Ruatan Street
Berwyn Heights, Md. 20740

Originally published 1989, 1998

Heritage Books by the Baltimore County Genealogical Society:

Abstracts of the Baltimore County Land Commissions, 1727–1762
Baltimore Cemeteries: Volume 5, St. Mary's Cemetery
Baltimore County Cemeteries: Volume 6, Mt. Olive
Tombstone Inscriptions of Govans Presbyterian Church Cemetery

International Standard Book Numbers
Paperbound: 978-1-58549-124-7
Clothbound: 978-0-7884-8977-8

INTRODUCTION

The Land Commission Records of Baltimore County from 1727 to 1762 are contained in two bound volumes (HWS #3, 1727-1737 and HWS & BB #4, 1737-1762) or on microfilm (R 112-3 and R 113-2) in the Maryland State Archives in Annapolis, Maryland. Researchers should be aware that land commissions are also found in the records of deeds. These have not been abstracted.

Information found in these land commission records relates to the appointment of persons (Commissioners) to investigate the requests of land owners or other interested parties (Petitioners) in the establishment, or re-defining, of lost, destroyed or otherwise unknown natural boundary markers (normally trees) of various tracts or parcels of land in colonial Baltimore County (which included part of present day Anne Arundel County and all of Harford County). The names of many early settlers who gave testimony (Deposition) to their knowledge of the land and its bounds are available to the genealogical researcher in these records. In almost every case the age of the deponent is given, and many of the depositions reveal other useful data such as names of fathers and mothers and other family members.

This information was abstracted by the late Dr. Richard Miller and donated to the Baltimore County Genealogical Society. His notes were spot-checked by the Publication Committee against the originals.

Committee members:

Robert W. Barnes
Patricia Czerniewski
Edward J. Goodman, Jr.
Edna A. Kanely
Eleanor C. Lukanich
Henry C. Peden, Jr.
Carol Porter
Martha Reamy
Shirley Reightler
F. Edward Wright

The Baltimore County Genealogical Society is greatly appreciative of the work of Dr. Miller and the members named above for compiling this signicant genealogical source book. We trust that our members, and other researchers, will find it useful in their research into early Baltimore County.

Henry C. Peden, Jr.
Vice President, BCGS
Chariman, Publications Committee

January, 1989

iii

1727-1737 (BOOK HWS NO. 3)

1. Petition of Michael MacNamara of Anne Arundel County:
1 March 1726/27: About 1696 the petitioner's father took up "Quinn" containing 500 acres in fork of Gunpowder River. Petitioner's father has since died and land descended to petitioner. (Page 1-3)
   Commissioners appointed 16 March 1726: Thomas Tolley, Nicholas Day, Luke Stansbury, and Archibald Rollo.
   Deposition of Charles Smith, 22 May 1727, age 70: Was at Annapolis when Thomas MacNamara asked the deponent if he knew of any clear land. He sold the land to Thomas MacNamara who sent James Crouch to survey it. Charles Smith went with him.

2. Petition of William Cromwell, Sr., March, 1726: In reference to "Mascall's Hope," containing 100 acres on the north side of the Patapsco River. (Page 4-6)
   Commissioners appointed 16 March 1726/27: Captain Lancelot Todd, John Orrick, Captain Benjamin Howard, and John Buck.
   Deposition of John Marsh, 13 May 1727, age about 60: About 50 years ago he was told by his master, John Cromwell, and John's brother William, and John Broad about the boundary.

3. Petition of Richard Gist, 10 March 1726/27: Owns two tracts on north side of Patapsco River called "Walton" and "Arden's Marsh," lying below the church. (Page 7-9)
   Commissioners appointed 10 March 1726: Captain Thomas Sheredine, William Buckner, Philip Jones and Richard Lenox.
   Deposition of Nicholas Hale, 1 January 1727/28, age 71: About 21 years ago he was shown the boundary of the two tracts by Joseph Strawbridge & Samuel Arding.

4. Petition of William Hammond, 9 June 1727: He and his minor brother own four tracts on north side of Patapsco River: "Spring Point," "Health," "Dearing's Increase," and "Hammond's Addition." (Page 10-14)
   Commissioners appointed 9 June 1727: Richard Gist, William Hamilton, Thomas Sheredine and Richard Owings.
   Deposition of John Hammond, 21 July 1727, age 34: About 24 years ago the deponent's father, Col. Thomas Hammond, was angry with some of his people for felling a boundary tree, and he told the deponent where the bounded trees of "Health" were.
   Deposition of Patrick Murphy, 21 July 1727, age 60: About 24 years ago Col. Thomas Hammond died.
   Deposition of Elizabeth Parker, 21 July 1727, aged about 42: About 30 years ago she was with Col. Thomas Hammond, Robert Parker and Job Evans at a bounded tree.
   Deposition of Richard Jones, 21 July 1727, aged about 50: About 24 years ago he was shown a bounded tree by Col. Thomas Hammond.
   Deposition of John Hooker, 21 July 1727, aged about 64: About 27 years ago he was shown a bounded tree by Col. Thomas Hammond.

5. Petition of Thomas Cross, 9 June 1727: Seized in right of his wife a parcel of land called "Hughes' Chance," surveyed 1 August 1669 for Joseph Hews for 150 acres, on west side of Bush River. (Page 15-19)
   Commissioners appointed 9 June 1727: James Presbury, Henry Wetherall, Thomas White and Aquila Hall.

Robert Robinson affixed notice on door of St. John's and also at St. George's Church.

Deposition of Edward Smith, 21 July 1727, aged about 70: About 50 years ago Thomas Heath and Thomas Preston told him in presence of Thomas Cross, Patrick Whayland, William Smith, Theophilus Jones and Mary Smith where his boundary was. Some years ago he sold an adjacent tract to William Smith.

6. Petition of Mary Marshall, widow, 3 August 1727: Seized of a parcel called "Goldsmith's Rest" surveyed on Spesutia Creek 16 July 1658 for her father, George Goldsmith. (Page 20-24)

Commissioners appointed in June, 1727: Garrett Garrettson, Francis Holland, John Clarke and Joseph Johnson.

Deposition of John Hall, Esq., 8 September 1727, age 70: About 1698 he married Martha Goldsmith, mother of the petitioner, and was shown a boundary tree near the mouth of Goufs Creek, opposite "a part of land known vulgarly as "Woodpeckers Hall," adjoining "Collingham." Mary Marshall married George Wells some few years ago.

7. Petition of Richard Galloway Sr. and Jr., of Anne Arundel County, 3 August 1727: Solomon Sparrow of Anne Arundel County left tract to Richard Galloway, after his death to Richard Galloway, Jr., called "Sparrows Nest," lying on a creek called Bare Creek (Bear Creek) formerly known as Broad Creek, on Patapsco River. (Page 25-29)

Commissioners appointed, November, 1727: Benjamin Bowen, John Gardner Clapham, Richard Lenox and Tobias Stansbury.

Deposition of Henry Jones, 27 February 1728, aged about 61: About 30 years ago well acquainted with "Sparrows Point."

Deposition of Jonas Brown, 27 February 1728, aged about 51: About 28 years ago he lived on a plantation called"Sparrows Point."

Deposition of John Eagleston, 27 February 1728, aged about 55: About 33 years ago the point known as the "Pasture Point" was esteemed to be the mouth of Bare Creek (Bear Creek).

Deposition of Richard Galt, 27 February 1728, aged about 37: About 11 or 12 years ago he lived on the plantation called "Sparrows Point."

8. Petition of Peter Galloway of Anne Arundel County, 3 August 1727: In reference to land in Patapsco Neck called "Howell" (alias "Powell") that was originally surveyed for Howell Powell of Talbot County. (Page 30-33)

Commissioners appointed: William Hamilton, Captain Thomas Sheredine, William Buckner and Luke Stansbury.

Deposition of Henry Jonas, 12 September 1727, aged about 61: About 24 years ago he met Charles Gorsuch, John Downs and Samuel Greening who knew the bounds. Henry Jonas also rented a cornfield of Gorsuch's on land called "Powell."

Deposition of Thomas Biddison, 12 September 1727, aged about 53: About 40 years ago this land was deemed to be Rigby's land. About 20 years ago he was informed by Charles Gorsuch that the land did not belong to Rigby but to Howell Powell.

Deposition not taken from James Jolly (Tolly?).

9. Petition of Abraham Cord and Thomas Cord, 18 November 1727: Their deceased father willed them two tracts, 100 acres each, on Swan Creek, called "French Plantation" and "Peter's Addition." (Page 34-37)

Commissioners appointed 30 April 1728: Edward Hall, John Hall, John Clarke and Bennett Garrett.

Deposition of William Cook, 1 May 1728, age 43: About 25 years ago Thomas Cord, Sr., father of petitioners, told him about a bounded red oak.

Deposition of Patrick Ruark, 1 May 1728, age 40: About 27 years ago he was a servant of Thomas Cord, Sr., and was living on "French Plantation" with his master. He also mentioned Lawrence Taylor, deceased.

10. Petition of Richard Smith of Calvert County, 9 March 1727: In reference to his owning one-half or one moiety of "Taskers Camp" and one moiety or one-half of "Bear Neck." (Page 38-42)

Commissioners appointed 2 April 1728: Thomas Tolley, Nicholas Day, Luke Stansbury and John Greer.

Deposition of Walter James, 2 July 1728, age about 34: About 7 years ago he went with John Taylor, Deputy Surveyor, who showed him the boundary tree of Walter Smith's land that ran to Cub Cabbin branch.

Deposition of Charles Smith, 2 July 1728, age about 70: About 30 years ago Col. Thomas Richardson told him that "Bear Neck" belonged to Walter Smith.

Deposition of Oliver Harriott, 2 July 1728, age about 51: Standing on south side of Gunpowder River near the falls and near a place called "New Port," John Taylor said he was with Col. Thomas Richardson when he bounded two trees on south side of Cub Cabbin branch, one for Walter Smith's "Bear Neck" and the other for Burgiss' "Cub Hill."

11. Petition of Nicholas Day, planter, 6 June 1728: Purchased "Sicklemore's Dock" formerly owned by Samuel Sicklemore, on the north side of the Gunpowder River. (Page 43-46)

Commissioners appointed: Daniel Scott, Thomas Tolley, Moses Groome and Archibald Rollo.

Deposition of John Fuller, 1 October 1728, age about 40: (St. John's Parish) About 27 years ago Robert Cutchin told him about the boundary.

Deposition of Thomas Cutchin, 1 October 1728, age about 51: His brother-in-law Samuel Sicklemore told him about the boundary.

12. Petition of William Hollis, 7 December 1728, St. George's Parish: In reference to owning 130 acres laid out by his father, William Hollis, on 1 August 1689 and called "Jeffrey's Neck," on the north side of Bush River. (Page 47-51)

Commissioners appointed: Roger Mathews, Aquilla Hall, John Clarke and George Drew.

Deposition of William Ozburn, 18 March 1728/9: About 26 years ago he was going down Bush River with William Hollis, Sr., fishing, opposite Abey Island.

13. Petition of Samuel Peele, Anne Arundel County merchant, 8 March 1728: In reference to his owning "Welches Adventure" on Gwyns Falls (bought from Henry Bateman). (Page 52-56)

Commissioners appointed: Richard Gist, George Walker, John Giles and Charles Ridgely.

Deposition of Nicholas Hale, Sr., 12 September 1729, age about 70: About 30 to 40 years ago Daniel Welch showed him the boundary. About 20 years ago Captain Thomas Larkin and John Holland told him the boundary.

Deposition of William Parrish, 12 September 1729, age about 50: About 20 years ago Robert Stocksdale showed him the boundary.

14. Petition of John Wilmot, 5 June 1729: In reference to his owning "Roberts Forrest" laid out by Thomas Roberts on 25 March 1703 for 500 acres on south side of the Gunpowder River. (Page 57-61)
   Commissioners appointed: Luke Stansbury, John Risteau, Nicholas Day and John Cockey.
   Deposition of Thomas Carr, 25 September 1729: He heard Joseph Gorsick (Gorsuch?) and John Cross, deceased, mention a bounded tree by a branch of Peterson's Run.
   Deposition of Captain John Boring, 25 September 1729: He heard John Wilmott mention the boundary about 20 years ago. Also mentioned John Cross being on the plantation with James Mathews.
   Deposition of Thomas Carr, 25 September 1729: About 17 years ago John Cross, deceased, and John Giles showed him the beginning tree of "Taylors Hall."
   Deposition of James Hedington, 25 September 1729: John Cross (deceased) had shown him the bounds.

15. ²Petition of William Smith, 9 September 1727: In reference to his owning tract called "Broom's Bloome" on head of Bush River. (Page 62-65)
   Commissioners appointed: John Hall, Esq., John Stokes, Daniel Scott and Richard Gist.
   Deposition of Simon Pierson (Pearson), 3 December 1728, age about 69 (in new dwelling of John Webster near a branch of Broad Run, and Bynum Run): About 27 years ago he and Robert Love were going home from Colonel Maxwell's plantation in the land of "Nodd" to his own plantation in Gunpowder Neck in woods near "Segley" by Broad Run. Robert Love showed him the boundary tree where three tracts came together: "Broom's Bloome," "Christopher's Camp," and "Segley," which had been shown him by Col. Thurston who used to go with the surveyor, Mr. Lightfoot.

16. Petition of Edmond Talbott, 5 June 1729: In reference to his owning two tracts: "Seneca Ridge" and "Talbott's Care," at the head of Bush River and adjoining tract "Hopewell" belonging to James Isham. (Page 66-70)
   Commissioners appointed: Thomas White, James Presbury, Henry Wetherall and Theophilus Jones.
   Deposition of John Hall, Esq., 7 October 1729, aged about 72: About 20 years ago he saw the boundary tree.
   Deposition of Thomas Norris, 7 October 1729, aged about 78: About 30 years ago Cornelius Herrington showed him the boundary tree.
   Deposition of Thomas Bond (Quaker), 7 October 1729, age about 51: About 30 years ago he was shown the boundary tree of Boothbuyes land.
   Witnesses: Edmond Talbott, James Isham and Nathaniel Sheppard.

17. Petition of Garrett Garrettson, 11 September 1729: In reference to owning "New Park" in St. George's Parish. (Page 71-75)
   Commissioners appointed: John Hall, Jr., John Clarke, Bennett Garrett and Aquila Paca.
   Deposition of Martin Deporte, 25 November 1729 aged 64: In 1701 he was carrying chain for Roger Mathews, dec'd., who showed him the bounded tree of "New Park" belonging to John Ew (?), gentleman.
   Deposition of Thomas Birchfield, 25 November 1729, aged 45: In 1717 Thomas Newsum and Samuel Jackson showed him the boundary.

18. Petition of Bartholomew Millhuse of Anne Arundel County, 11 September 1729: In reference to his owning tract called "The Forrest" on the head of Salt Peter Creek. (Page 76-79)

Commissioners appointed: Luke Raven, Thomas Tolley, John Scott and William Galloway.

Deposition of Oliver Harold, 17 February 1729/30, aged about 53: About 30 years ago Giles Stephens showed him the boundary tree of Donse's lands, with Daniel Scott.

Deposition of Michael Rutledge, 17 February 1729/30, aged about 34: He lived with Daniel Scott, Sr. and often heard Daniel Scott speak of the tree.

19. Petition of Benjamin Jones, 3 February 1729/1730: He owns 200 acres of "Friendship" near Gunpowder River. (Page 80-84)

Commissioners appointed: Richard Caswell, William Smith, James Presbury and James Maxwell.

Deposition of John Armstrong, 28 February 1729/1730, aged about 49: About 15 or 16 years ago Jane Hicks, widow of William, showed him the boundary. About 8 or 10 years ago John Brooks and William and James Hicks showed him the boundary.

20. Petition of James Isham, 11 November 1729: To again prove bounds of his land "Hopewell" since those who testified to Edmond Talbott's commission did not swear to testimony. (Page 85-88)

Commissioners appointed: Thomas White, James Presbury, Henry Wetherall and Theophilus Jones.

Deposition of Cadwallader Jones, 8 January 1729/1730, aged about 59: About 33 years ago Cornelius Herrington showed him the boundary.

Deposition of Thomas Norris, 8 January 1729/1730, aged about 78: He says his previous testimony was in error and he agrees with Cadwallader Jones.

21. Petition of Isaac Johns of Calvert County, 11 August 1729: Some years ago he and brother Kensey Johns bought "Christopher's Camp." William Smith's commission made a mistake to prejudice claim of Isaac Johns and claim of deceased brother. (Page 89-96)

Commissioners appointed: Thomas White, Dr. Josias Middlemore, Daniel Scott and Henry Garrett.

Deposition of Antell Deaver, 12 May 1730, age about 40: About 23 years ago he lived with John Webster as an apprentice; so did Thomas Litten. Land adjoined "Sedgely."

Deposition of John Webster, 12 May 1730, age about 64: About 24 years ago Robert Love came and said he had been employed to find land called "My Lord's Gift" and knows the boundary of this land.

22. Petition of John Bowen, 11 June 1730: In reference to owning "Wellcome" on Back River. (Page 97-98)

Commissioners appointed: Thomas Todd, Philip Jones and John Eaglestone.

Deposition of John Wilmoth, 27 July 1730, age about 48: About 28 years Charles Gorsuch, who took up the land, showed him the boundary.

Deposition of Robert Green, 27 July 1730, age about 35: Gave a similar statement regarding boundary.

Deposition of Isaac Sampson, 27 July 1730, age about 60: Was with old Rowland Thornbury who showed him the beginning tree of David Adams' land.

23. Petition of John Clark and Mary Forester, 6 March 1729/30: They own 400 acre tract "Carter's Rest" on Muskeeto Creek. (He owns 310 acres and she owns 90 acres.) (Page 99-103)

Commissioners appointed: John Hall, Jr., Bennett Garrett, John Stokes and Aquila Paca.

Deposition of Thomas Morris, 27 June 1730, age about 60: About 40 years ago he was servant to Laowdeweck (Ludowick) Martin who owned part of "Carter's Rest."

Deposition of John Hall, Esq., 27 June 1730, age about 72: About 30 years ago there was a dispute among the owners of "Carter's Rest."

24. Petition of Thomas Stone, 4 June 1730: He owns 100 acre tract "Olive Yard" in Patapsco Neck. (Page 104-106)

Commissioners appointed: William Buckner, Thomas Todd, Benjamin Bowen and John Bowen.

Deposition of Edward Maham, age about 46: About 11 or 12 years ago he was with Samuel Hornton and Col. John Dorsey the surveyor.

25. Petition of George Godwin, 8 August 1730: He owns tracts "Margrett's Delight" and "Comes Adventure" (126 acres) on a branch of the Patapsco River. (Page 107-111)

Commissioners appointed: William Hammond, Charles Randall, Jr., Charles Ridgely and George Buchanan.

Deposition of John Hurd, 29 October 1730, age about 24: About 6 years ago he was with Robert Parker, deceased, and was shown the boundary.

Deposition of Jacob Hurd, 29 October 1730, age 26: About 10 years ago he lived with Robert Parker and he showed him the boundary.

26. Petition of Francis Bucknel and Henry Bucknel, 11 November 1730: Their father, Thomas, by his last will and testament, bequeathed them a 100 acre tract called "Contest" on Swan Creek. (Page 112-117)

Commissioners appointed: John Clark, Bennett Garrett, Samuel Howell and Abraham Cord.

Deposition of Garret Garrison, 20 January 1730/31, age about 58: About 25 years ago the land called "Easey Hill" belonged to Capt. Henry Johnson and is now known as "Contest."

Deposition of Thomas Gash, 20 January 1730/31, age 39: About 24 years age he was with Capt. Lawrence Draper and was shown the boundary.

Deposition of Elizabeth Cottrell, 20 January 1730/31, age 63: About 32 years ago her husband John settled near "Contest."

Deposition of Thomas Morris, 20 January 1730/31, age 60: Heard old Richard Prekins (?) about 40 years ago speak of this land.

Deposition of Thomas Mitchell, 20 January 1730/31, age 46: About 30 years ago he heard about this land.

Deposition of William Cook, 20 January 1730/31, age 46: About 30 years ago he heard his father-in-law, Emanuel Seeley, speak of this land.

27. Petition of Mary Talbot (Tolbot), widow, of Anne Arundel County, 17 March 1730: Her husband John, by his last will and testament, bequeathed to sons John and Edward (now minors) two tracts in Baltimore County: "Barrett's Delight" (200 acres) and "Barrett's Addition" (190 ac.) (Page 118-122)

Commissioners appointed: Luke Stansbury, John Kister, John Cockey and Abraham Vaughan.

Deposition of John Wilmott, 20 May 1731, age about 40: About 16 years ago John Barrett showed him the boundary on Wilkinson's Run, adj. "Taylor's Hall."

28. Petition of Morgan and Jabez Murray, 17 March 1730: In reference to 500 acre tract called "Morgan's Delight." (Page 123-128)
    Commissioners appointed: William Hamilton, John Risteau, George Buchanan and John Cockey.
    Deposition of Josephias Murray, 18 May 1731: When he was a child about 30 years ago his father and father-in-law, Thomas Cromwell, showed him the boundary.
    Deposition of Samuel Hooker (Quaker), 18 May 1731, aged about 44: About 17 years ago his father, Thomas Hooker, showed him the boundary. About 16 years ago Capt. Bond, Dutton Lane and Col. Hammond showed him the boundary. Hooker's and Stevenson's lands adjoined it.
    Deposition of Samuel Merriman, 18 May 1731, age about 48: About 24 years ago he was shown the boundary.
    Deposition of Samuel Hooker, 18 May 1731: About 27 years ago Dutton Lane showed him James Murray's land. About 29 years ago Thomas Hooker and Nicholas Hall showed him the land adjoining Benjamin Bowen, "Friend's Discovery" owned by Mr. Raven.
    Deposition of Richard Cooker, 18 May 1731, aged about 30: About 22 years ago he was shown the bounds.

29. Petition of Bethia Calvert, 5 November 1731: In reference to "Watertown" in Gunpowder Neck on south side of Bush River. (Page 129-131)
    Commissioners appointed: Nicholas Day, Robert Robertson, William Barney and William Smith.
    Deposition of Simon Pearson, 2 April 1731, aged about 71: His mother-in-law, Margaret Anlis, showed him the bounds near the mouth of Watertown Creek.
    Deposition of John Dawney, 2 April 1731, aged about 37: Francis Dallahide showed him the bounds.

30. Petition of Robert Robertson, 26 November 1731: In reference to 150 acre tract "Hogg Neck" on south side of Bush River near the mouth of Bow Creek. (Page 132-134)
    Commissioners appointed: James Presbury, Henry Wetherall, Theophilus Jones and James Maxwell.
    Deposition of John Sumner, 2 March 1731, aged about 45: About 12 years ago Cornelius Herrington showed him the boundary opposite Tapl (?) Point.
    Deposition of Zachariah Smith, 2 March 1731, aged about 30: Patrick Wayland said his father, Henry Mathews (?), showed him the boundary.
    Deposition of William Rhodes, 2 March 1731, aged about 38: Gave a statement regarding bounds.

31. Petition of Garrett Garrettson, 2 November 1731: In reference to his part of a 300 acre tract called "Oakinton" on the bay between the mouth of Swan Creek and Susquehanna River. The other part belonged to Thomas Brown, deceased. (Page 135-139)
    Commissioners appointed: John Clark, Bennett Garrett, John Stokes and Aquila Paca.
    Deposition of Thomas Mitchell, 5 June 1732, aged about 48: About 31 years ago he was servant to Garrett Garrettson and lived on land adjoining "Martin's Rest." Richard Simpson told him about the boundary land.

Deposition of Archibald Buchanan, 5 June 1732, age about 26: About 16 years ago his father, Archibald Buchanan, bought "Martin's Rest."

Deposition of John Hall, Esq., 5 June 1732, age 74: About 36 years ago he sold part of "Oakinton" beginning at the mouth of Swan Creek to Thomas Brown, deceased.

Deposition of Thomas Simpson, 10 April 1732, aged about 42: About 28 years ago his father Richard Simpson showed him the boundary land.

Deposition of William Simpson, 10 April 1732, aged about 37: About 28 years ago his father Richard Simpson showed him the boundary land.

32. Petition of Tobias Stansbury, 11 March 1731: In reference to "Nell's Delight" on north side of Bare (Bear) Creek of Patapsco River. (Page 140-143)

Commissioners appointed: Philip Jones, Thomas Sheredine, John Eaglestone and Luke Trotten.

Deposition of Benjamin Bowen, 25 May 1732, aged about 52: He lived for 40 years within two miles of where he now stands: "The cove which is the first cove that makes out of branch of Bare Creek which leads up between this deponent's dwelling plantation and the new dwelling plantation of Tobias Stansbury and on east side of said branch was known as "Bull Neck Cove" and land to the northward of said cove was Ralph Nell's land."

Deposition of John Bowen, 25 May 1732, aged about 45: He made a statement similar to Benjamin Bowen above.

Deposition of Jonas Robinson, 25 May 1732, aged about 35: Made a statement similar to Benj. Bowen.

33. Petition of John Baldwin and William Rumsey, Cecil County, 10 June 1732: In reference to "Heathcoats Cottage" in Baltimore County between two main falls of the Gunpowder River, surveyed 22 March 1678 for Nathaniel Heathcoat of Anne Arundel County; containing 500 acres. (Page 144-148)

Commissioners appointed: Thomas Tolley, Richard Caswell, William Low and Humphrey Wells Stokes.

Deposition of John Roberts alias Campble, 29 August 1732, aged about 41: About 20 years ago his father-in-law John Campble heard of great drain of third branch on northside of Gunpowder River. James Richardson, son of Col. Thomas Richardson, formerly surveyor of Baltimore County, knew boundary of Thompson's land and Nicholas Gassaway's land.

Deposition of John Green, 29 August 1732, aged about 47: About 14-15 years ago his uncle, John Taylor (an ancient person), formerly deputy surveyor of Baltimore County, showed him the boundary adjoining Nicholas Day's plantation.

34. Petition of Gabriel Brown, 10 June 1732: In reference to "Brown's Entrance" on the upper branches of Swan Creek. (Page 149-151)

Commissioners appointed: Aquila Paca, Edward Hall, William Bradford and Jarvis Gilbert.

Deposition of John Hall, Esq., 28 October 1732, age 74: About 1700 he took up "Hall's Plains" on the north side of the west branch of Swan Creek, adjoining "Abbott."

Deposition of Robert West, Sr., 28 October 1732, age about 63: About 7-8 years ago Edward Wheelbourne, now deceased, showed him the bounded tree of Thomas Brown's land.

Deposition of William Wheelbourne, 28 October 1732, age about 24: About 7-8 years ago his father, Edward Wheelbourne, deceased, showed him the bounded tree.

Deposition of Thomas Wheelbourne, 28 October 1732, age about 31: Same as his brother William.

35. Petition of William Bradford, 10 June 1732: About 3 years ago he escheated a tract on Binam (Bynum) Run called "Plasterer's Hall" now called "Bradford's Barrens." (Page 152-154)
Commissioners appointed: Thomas White, Parker Hall, Nicholas Day and Benjamin Jones.
Deposition of Charles Whiteacre, 7 October 1732, age about 37: About 20 years ago the deponent, his father (John Whiteacre), John Nicholson (commonly called Jack the Danber, and who claimed "Plasterer's Hall"), and deponent's brother, Peter, all saw the boundary land.
Deposition of Peter Whiteacre, 7 October 1732, age about 35: Same statement as his brother Charles.
Deposition of Thomas Bond (Quaker), 7 October 1732, age about 53: About 26 years ago "on a communication between Thomas Bond, Aquila Paca (deceased), John Whiteacre, Sr. (deceased father of Charles and Peter Whiteacre)" he knew about the bounds of the land he was about to buy from Aquila Paca.

36. Petition of Thomas Hines, 10 June 1732: In reference to tract "Come By Chance" on northeast creek of Back River. (Page 155-157)
Commissioners appointed: Thomas Sheredine, Peasly Ingram, Luke Stansbury and Thomas Dulany.
Deposition of John Boreing, 7 July 1732, age about 50: When he was about 11 years old his father-in-law, John Ferry, took up "Come By Chance."
Deposition of Thomas Biddeson, 7 July 1732, age about 58: About 28 years ago he asked Andrew Anderson about John Ferry's land.
Deposition of John Harryman, 7 July 1732, age about 38: About 16 years ago he knew of John Ferry's land and John Boreing's land.
Deposition of Walter James, 7 July 1732, age about 39: Gave statement similar to John Harryman.

37. Petition of Peasly Ingram, gentleman, 10 June 1732: In reference to 475 acre tract called "Holly Neck." (Page 158-161)
Commissioners appointed: Thomas Sheredine, Thomas Todd, Thomas Stansbury and Philip Jones.
Deposition of Richard Lenox, 6 July 1732, age about 52: About 23 years ago at Robert Gardner's house at "Wellses Neck" at the mouth of creek at Cedar Island, James Cooke bounded the tree at Breezy Point.

38. Petition of Edward Cantwell, 10 June 1732: Samuel Jackson's last will and testament bequeathed to Sara Hie (now wife of Edward Cantwell) a 100 acre tract called "The Hazard" near "The Levell." (Page 162-165)
Commissioners appointed: John Clarke, George Drew, Bennett Garrett and William Osbourn.
Deposition of Martin Depost, 7 October 1732, age about 68: About 36 years ago Samuel Jackson (who took up the land "Hazard") saw Col. Thomas Richardson bound the tree. (The Court asked if Martin Depost was in his proper senses, and asked for more proof.)
Deposition of Thomas Williamson, 23 February 1732, age about 37: Said he knew of the bounded tree.
Deposition of Samuel Brown, 23 February 1732, age about 40: Said he knew of the bounded tree.

39. Petition of John Steward of Anne Arundel County, 7 March 1731/32: In reference to "Newtown" on north side of Gwin's Falls. (Page 166-177)
Commissioners appointed: William Hammond, John Moale, George Walker and Charles Ridgely. (Charles Ridgely owned contiguous land and was not satisfied by the Commission's inquiry. He referred to testimony of William Parrish on land where Peter Bond lives, and to testimony of Elinor Savage. He requested the report be suppressed; so ruled.)
Commissioners appointed 10 June 1732: Richard Gist, William Hamilton, John Risteau and Chris. Randall, Sr.
Deposition of William Hammond, 10 June 1732, age about 32: On 19 July 1731 John Snow said when he was a servant of Peter Bond about 20 years ago, Peter Bond showed him the beginning tree of the tract he had with his wife and said it might be questioned after his death. (Written deposition of John Moale was also mentioned.)
Deposition of Stephen Gill, 10 June 1732, age about 60: Peter Bond showed him the bounded tree of his land. He owns 70-80 acres of "Parishes Range" which he bought of William Parish adjoining "Newtown."
Deposition of Elinor Savage, 10 June 1732, age about 50: Her husband Peter Bond showed her the bounds. When Peter Bond first settled land James Carroll said he was settled on his land, but Peter Bond had Charles Gorsuch swear before Thomas Beale as to bounded tree, and James Carroll never molested her or husband. She sold land with her husband Hill Savage.
Deposition of Edward Roberts, 10 June 1732, age about 59: About 30 years ago he was living by Gwin's Falls where Dr. Charles Carroll's mill now stands and saw old Peter Bond who said he was looking for the beginning boundary tree of Richard Gwin's land which now belonged to his son Peter.
Deposition of William Parish (Quaker), 10 June 1732, age about 54: About 18-19 years ago he was catching herrings in Gwin's Falls with Peter Bond who showed him the bound tree of land he lived on. He never owned land contiguous to "Newtown," but he did own part of "Parishes Range."
Deposition of Richard Gist, 10 June 1732, age about 49: Sometime ago he was on Commission relating to the land of Samuel Peel between Jones Falls and here. William Parish volunteered information but it was felt he was trying to "baffle Nicholas Hail's evidences." Robert Stockdale had told him the boundary. Part of "Parishes Range" adjoining "Newtown" is owned by John Parish, a nephew of William.
Deposition of Charles Wells, 10 June 1732, age about 30: About 14-15 years ago Joseph Parkinson, then servant to Peter Bond, knew of the boundary.
Deposition of Thomas Taylor, 10 June 1732, age about 54: About 20 years ago, Peter Bond showed him the bounds.
Deposition of Charles Ridgely, 10 June 1732, age 30: About two months ago he was on the Commission to examine bounds of "Newtown." Thomas Hooker (Quaker) was involved.
Deposition of Christopher Randall, 10 June 1732, age about 53: About a year ago he heard Thomas Hooker say he and James Murray knew "Parishes Range" and the beginning tree of Gwin's land.
Deposition of William Hamilton, 10 June 1732, age about 50: Same statement as Christopher Randall above.
Deposition of William Bond, 11 June 1733, age about 48: About 30 years ago James Carroll told Peter Bond, who was seating land he had by his wife, he better decline seating then and he would let him have same and show him land elsewhere; Peter Bond declined. Later, William Bond saw Charles Gorsuch swear before magistrate Thomas Beale regarding the beginning tree of land Peter Bond had by wife which was taken up by her father, Richard Gwin, a

little below John Parish's plantation. The old men, Charles Gorsuch and Isaac Jackson, said that old Richard Gwin was one of the takers up of the land; brother Peter came by land with his wife, Gwin's daughter, about 27 years ago, a little plantation settled by George Ogg. His brother Peter also took up land further up the Falls, part of which he later sold to John Wells. Peter Bond built house on "Newtown" for himself and let his father and mother live in house he first built on the said land.

Deposition of William Rogers, age about 29, also taken, regarding his knowledge of the bounds.

40. Petition of William Hollis, 9 March 1732: In reference to eight tracts on east side of Bush River near its mouth: "Islington" ("Islenton"), "Ellinge" ("Upper Eleing"), "Hollis' Refuse," "Holly Hill," "Hollis' Chance," "Swampy Point," "Howell's Nest," and "Painter's Neglect." Page 178-184)

Commissioners appointed: Roger Mathews, Bennett Garrett, John Clarke and George Drew.

Deposition of Benjamin Hanson, 3 October 1733, age about 40: About 10 years ago William Renolds formerly lived on the plantation and showed him the bounds.

Deposition of William Osburn, 3 October 1733, age about 48: About 30 years ago William Hollis, father of this William Hollis, showed him the bounds.

Deposition of Symon Pearson, 3 October 1733, age 73: In 1684 he was at house of William Hollis, Sr. with Samuel Jackson, Robert Gaskin, and others who knew the bounds.

Deposition of John Debruler, 3 October 1733, age 60: About 33 years ago he was with his father at the house of William Hollis, Sr. and he knew of the bounds.

Deposition of John Hall, Esq., 3 October 1733, age 76: About 50 years ago the land was given to grandfather of William Hollis by Sampson, but because of some deficiency in Sampson's will, Hollis' grandfather escheated the land, and Hollis grandmother was then living where William Hollis now lives.

Deposition of Thomas Norris in October, 1733, at house of Francis Ogg. Deponent, age 84, said about 30 years ago, coming down Bush River in boat with Cornelius Herrington, the land in question was in possession of John Parker, a tenant of William Hollis, Sr.

Deposition of Symon Pearson in October, 1733, at house of Francis Ogg. Deponent, age 73, said about 33 years ago, at plantation where Francis Ogg now lives, it was then in possession of John Parker, Sr., tenant of William Hollis, Sr.

41. Petition of Luke Trotten and Jacob Rowles, 9 June 1733: In reference to four tracts: "Walton's Neck," "Gorden's Marsh," "Addition to Walton," and "Martaineson." (Page 185-188)

Commissioners appointed: Thomas Todd, Robert North, Benjamin Bowen and Buckler Partridge.

Deposition of Tobias Stansbury, June, 1733, age about 42: Samuel Ardin told him about the bounds on the south side of Bush River and in reference to "Martin's Neck."

Deposition of Luke Stansbury, June, 1733, age about 45: Gave statement similar to Tobias Stansbury above. Deposition of William Lynch, June, 1733, age about 26: His mother said she believed Nicholas Hale had proved the bounds of "Walton" in the wrong place because she heard her deceased husband Robuck Lynch say so.

11

42. Petition of Thomas Todd, 8 June 1733: In reference to two tracts in Patapsco Neck: "Old Road" and "Thurrell's Neck." (Page 189-193)
Commissioners appointed: Thomas Sheredine, Philip Jones, Luke Trotten and Richard Lenox.
Deposition of Henry Jonas, 12 August 1733, age 66: About 33 years ago Philip Lines said he had bought the right of "Old Road" from Thomas Thomas and William Batten, and had jury on land to prove bounds. After jury had gone Richard Simpson, Nicholas Hale, John Hayes and deponent went to bounded tree on Hallowing Point.
Deposition of Isaac Sampson, 8 June 1733, age 61: Father told him when he was a small boy about the bounded land on Thurrell's Creek.
Deposition of John Harryman, 8 June 1733, age 39: William Farfer told him about the boundary.

43. Petition of Philip Jones, Jr., 6 June 1733: In reference to two tracts in Patapsco Neck: "Johnson" and "Thomas' Addition." (Page 194-195)
Commissioners appointed: Thomas Todd, Robert North, Benjamin Bowen and Buckler Partridge.
Deposition of Henry Jonas, November, 1733, age 66: The year he came on "Johnson" he heard the sons of Thomas Durbin say where the bounds were.
Deposition of Richard Gardner, November, 1733, age about 23: When he lived with Joseph Lobb he heard about the bounds of Durbin's land.
Deposition of Nicholas Fitzsimons, November, 1733, age 76: He carried the chain when Richardson surveyed Durbin's land.

44. Petition of Benjamin Jones of Baltimore County, in behalf of Thomas Harwood of Prince George's County, 18 Sept.1733: In reference to a tract called "Lyon" on south side of the Gunpowder River. (Page 196-198)
Commissioners appointed: Richard Caswell, Edward Day, William Bradford and Thomas Dulany.
Deposition of John Bevans, June, 1734, age about 53: About 40 years ago his father, John Bevans, late of Baltimore County, showed him the bounds.

45. Petition of Henry Garrett, Isaac Butterworth and Daniel Scott, Jr., 15 November 1733: In reference to three tracts that depend on bounds of John Hall's "Jericho." (Page 199-201)
Commissioners appointed: Thomas Warren, John Durbin, Robert Clark and Jarvis Gilbert.
Deposition of Thomas Shie, 25 February 1733/4, age about 54: Said "Jericho" adjoined Hall's "Rich Neck."
Witnesses were Daniel Scott, Sr. and Henry Garrett.

46. Petition of John Crockett, 16 November 1733: In reference to three tracts: "Brodwell's Hills," "Samuel's Hills" and "Smith Range." (Page 202-204)
Commissioners appointed: Henry Wetherall, Robert Robertson, Humphrey Wells Stokes and Theophilus Jones.
Deposition of James Isham, 30 March 1734, age about 62: About 30 years ago Cornelius Herrington and Thomas Preston showed him the bounds on the south side of the southwest branch of Bush River.
Deposition of Charles Baker, 30 March 1734, age about 63: About 20 years ago James Isham showed him the bounds.

47. Petition of William Green, 9 March 1733/4: In reference to a tract called "Coale's Addition." (Pages 205-207)

Commissioners appointed: George Buchanan, William Rogers, Charles Ridgely and John Edwards.

Deposition of John Coale, Sr., 30 May 1734, age about 65: On west side of Monntenay's Run he bounded tree by order of Col. Thomas Richardson.

Deposition of Charles Gorsuch, 30 May 1734, age about 64, gave a statement similar to the above.

48. Petition of William Maccomas and Daniel Maccomas, 9 June 1734: In reference to a 200 acre tract on Winter's Run called "Gresham's Colledge," which was part of a 500 acre tract granted to John Gresham. (Page 208-213)

Commissioners appointed: Thomas White, Daniel Scott, Jr., Benjamin Norris and William ---.

Deposition of Thomas Bond (Quaker) 8 July 1734, age about 55: About 30 years ago, shortly after he settled where he now lives, Capt. Thomas Preston and his son Thomas showed him the bounded tree of "Gibson's Park." About 12 years later Thomas Bale, who married the sister of Robert Gibson, said Robert Gibson said he was not present when his father took up the land. Aquila Paca, deceased, purchased "Gibson's Park," near mouth of Paca's "Spring Branch," adjoining land laid out for David Lawrence and land laid out for --- Doyns. Thomas Bond and brother W. Bond with Aquila Paca ran lines of "Gibson's Park" and found that Thomas Bond's land was not in "Gibson's Park," but land where Thomas Preston, Jr. lived was in "Gibson's Park." Later, Thomas Bond ran course of adjoining tract "Claggett's Forest" adjoining "Scott's Lott." Aquila Paca said "that for as much as the said Thomas Preston was a roague and in all probability would steal the hoggs that he....." (no further abstraction, but apparently he was challenging Preston's credibility). Later, Aquila Paca, and Thomas Preston referred the matter to Daniel Scott, James Harris, Roger Mathews, John Webster and Moses Groom.

49. Petition of Humphrey Wells Stokes, 16 May 1734: Col. George Wells' last will and testament bequeathed to daughter Susannah Mary Stokes, mother of Humphrey Wells Stokes, a small part of "Collett's Point" and part of 250 acre "Planter's Delight", now called "Stoney Point." (Page 214)

Commissioners appointed: Roger Mathews, John Hall, Jr., Edward Wakeman and Bennett Garrett.

Deposition of John Greer, 18 September 1734, age about 48: Richard Smithers once owned land and said Edward Moore told him he bounded a tree by order of Col. George Wells near house where Madame Wells now lives. (Page 214)

50. Petition of Robert Wilkinson, 30 November 1734: In reference to 425 acre tract called "Landesell" on the east side of Bare Creek. (Page 216-219)

Commissioners appointed: Thomas Todd, Luke Trotten, Robert North and Benjamin Bowen, Sr.

Deposition of Zachariah Gray, 1 March 1734, age about 34: Said that he and Philip Pitstow know the bounds (Robert Wilkinson objected).

Deposition of John Eagleston, 1 March 1734, age about 60: Said Philip Pitstow & Tamar Linix showed him the bounds.

Deposition of Thomas Biddison, 1 March 1734 age about 62: About 34-35 years ago he & Robert Wilkinson knew bounds.

Deposition of Luke Trotten, 1 March 1734, age about 40: About 8-9 years ago Thomas Felps said Tamar Linix knew the bounds (and showed him).

Deposition of Jacob Rowles, 1 March 1734, age about 47: Tamar Linix told him the bounds of her land.

Deposition of Thomas Sheredine, 1 March 1734, age about 35: About 3-4 years ago Richard Lennox showed him the bounds. (Page 216-219)

51. Petition of George Ogg, 7 June 1735: In reference to a tract called "The Rich Levell." (Page 220-222)

Commissioners appointed: Richard Gist, Christopher Gist, Josephus Murray and Henry Butler.

9 July 1735: Set up notices at St. Paul's Church and Patapsco Ferry.

Deposition of Joshua Howard, 1 August 1735, age about 70: About 30 years ago Andrew Hurd was the original taker up of the land.

52. Petition of Robert Mason of St. Mary's County, 15 May 1734: In reference to 490 acre tract called "Paradise" granted to his grandfather Thomas Mason, on branch of Swan Creek. (Page 223-226)

Commissioners appointed: Aquila Paca, Bennett Garrett, John Clark and Michael Gilbert.

Deposition of Edward Hall, gentleman, 6 July 1734, age about 40: About 2 years ago George Morgan said he was present at the bounding of the first tree of Richard Perkins' land "Paradise."

Deposition of Thomas Mitchell, 6 July 1734, age about 52: About 12 years ago he was present at the bounding of land ("Paradise"). George Morgan now deceased. Perkins sold land to Robert Mason.

53. Petition of Oliver Cromwell, 8 August 1734: In reference to "Cromwell's Chance" (part has been sold). (Page 227-228)

Commissioners appointed: George Buchanan, John Riston (Ristean), Charles Ridgely and Solomon Wooder.

Deposition of Henry Butler, 20 December 1734 and 19 July 1735, age about 64: He was one of the chain carriers when surveyor laid out land. James Murray said he would lay out here Dr. Rattenbury's warrant for 500 acres and call the land "Gallipott Levell." Thomas Cromwell cut "TC" in one side of tree for "Cromwell's Chance" and James Murray cut "IR" on other side for Dr. Rattenbury.

54. Petition of Robert Courtney, 16 May 1734: In reference to tract called "Hammond's Hope." (Page 229-231)

Commissioners appointed: Aquila Paca, John Hall, Jr., John Clarke and Bennett Garrett.

Deposition of John Hall, Esq. 22 July 1734, age about 76: In 1684 he saw people at head of Swan Creek close to main road going down to Herring Run lay out "North Yarmouth," adjoining "Hammond's Hope."

Deposition of Edward Hall, gentleman, 22 July 1734, age about 40: Gave a statement similar to John Hall above.

Deposition of Thomas Mitchell, 22 July 1734 age about 52: About 20 years ago George Morgan showed him the bounded tree of "Brands" so called because it was seated by Samuel Brand.

Deposition of Garrett Garison, 22 July 1734, age 60: About 30 years ago he was shown the boundary of land.

55. Petition of Robert North, 3 June 1736: In reference to two tracts in Patapsco Neck: "The Plains" and "Philip's Addition." (Page 232-235)

Commissioners appointed: Thomas Sheredine, Philip Jones, John Bowen and Benjamin Bowen.

Deposition of John Eagleston, 13 July 1736, age about 62: About 30 years ago John Francis Holland said that Captain Thomas Roberts, a tenant to Samuel Thomas, told him that tree by Bear Creek in Chinkopin Neck was the bounded tree of Samuel Thomas' land.

Deposition of Edward Sweeting, 13 July 1736, age 26: John Francis Holland showed him the bounded tree.

Deposition of Thomas Sheredine, 13 July 1736, age 37: About 5-6 years ago John Francis Holland told him the boundary.

Deposition of Benjamin Bowen, 13 July 1736, age about 54: About 38 years ago he heard his father speak of boundary of "Philip's Addition" in Bull Neck.

Deposition of John Bowen, 13 July 1736, age about 59: About 4 years ago he heard about Philip Thomas' land.

Deposition of Patrick Lynch, 13 July 1736, age 38: About 6-7 years ago Jonas Bowen showed him Samuel Thomas's land in Bull Neck.

56. Petition of John Dorrumple, 6 March 1735: In reference to part of "The Friendship" on west side of Susquehannah River. (Page 236)

Commissioners appointed: Nathan Rigbie, Thomas Warren, Charles Worthington and Jacob Giles.

Deposition of Frances Foy, 22 September 1736, age 60: 36 years ago she heard Richard Perkins, Sr., deceased, say that Harrisons land bounded land called "Itrupt" on northwest side of Rork(?) Run, and her husband Daniel Johnson said that Harrison's land came to the southeast corner tree of "Itrupt" and she heard Richard Perkins say that Col. Thomas Taylor's land came to same corner.

Deposition of Richard Perkins, 22 September 1736, age 55: 36 years ago he heard father Richard Perkins speak of the boundary (similar statement as France Foy).

57. Petition of Josias Middlemore, 6 March 1735: In reference to several tracts: "Palmer Point" on west side of Swan Creek; "Swan Harbour" on Swan Creek; "Palmer's Forrest" on branches of Cranberry Swamp and head of Rumley Creek; "Fanny's Inheritance" on west side of Swan Creek (in right of his wife); and "Raley" or "Raly." Also mentioned "Gouldsmith's Enlargement." (Page 240-244)

Commissioners appointed: Aquila Paca, John Hall, Jr., Parker Hall and Edward Wakeman.

Deposition of John Hall, Esq. 24 June 1736, age about 79: About 1694, riding with wife Martha and Thomas Brown, he was shown the bounded tree of "Oakington" and 23 years ago he ran out "Swan Harbour" beginning at the same tree, near branch of Swan Creek called The Little Run.

Deposition of John Clark, 24 June 1736, age about 50: About 20 years ago he was shown the bound tree of Palmers land. Lawrence Draper showed him the bound tree of "Swan Harbour." He was then surveyor of Baltimore County and wished to purchase "Swan Harbour" himself, so he was very careful.

Deposition of William Sympson, 24 June 1736, age about 41: About 20 years ago he was shown bound tree by father Richard Sympson or by uncle Thomas Gilbert, adjoining "Oakington" and near plantation on bay now in possession of Elizabeth Smith, widow.

Deposition of Garrett Garrettson, 24 June 1736, age about 60: About 49 years ago he rode with Thomas Brown who showed him the boundary.

Deposition of John Clark, 24 June 1736, age about 50: On 5 May 1717, being surveyor of Baltimore County, he was laying out land for John Baley who said Samuel Jackson or Thomas Cord or William Cooke showed him tree as beginning of Palmer's land ("Palmer's Forrest").

Deposition of Thomas Williams, 24 June 1736, age about 42: About 11 years ago William Cook and John Baley showed him the beginning tree of Dr. Middlemore's land. Henry Chatham also showed him the boundary.

Deposition of Lucy Williams, 24 June 1736, age about 38. About 4 years ago Henry Chatham showed her the boundary.

Deposition of Thomas Bond, 24 June 1736, age about 57: About 10 years ago John Baley and Thomas Birchfield showed him the boundary of "Palmer's Forrest."

Deposition of John Clark, 31 July 1736, age about 50: As surveyor of Baltimore County in 1714, he came with Lawrence Draper to run line of "Palmer's Point."

Deposition of John Hall, Esq., 31 July 1736, age about 79: In 1694-1695 with Emanuell Coty he was shown the bounded tree of "Palmer's Point" and "Gouldsmith's Enlargement."

Witnesses: Dr. Middlemore, Garrett Garrettson, Samuel Howell, William Dallam, Bennett Garrett, Major Thomas White (not all of these men were at all of the depositions however).

58. Petition of Samuel Griffith, 6 March 1735: In reference to 2 tracts: "Leaf's Junior" and "Polecat." (Page 245-258)

Commissioners appointed: Aquila Paca, Parker Hall, Roger Mathews and John Clark.

Deposition of Roger Mathews, 29 July 1736, age about 50: About 20 years ago with James Phillips he was shown the land of F. Leaf, now in possession of Samuel Griffith on Lumley's Run.

Deposition of Absalom Brown, 29 July 1736, age not given: About 17-18 years ago with brother Samuel Brown on road from Henry Millan's toward James Phillips, Samuel Brown pointed out bounded tree of Leaf's land and also James Phillips, as told him by deceased father, Samuel Brown.

Deposition of Benjamin Henson, 29 July 1736, age about 46: About 28-29 years ago, his father Thomas Henson was interested in buying "Leaf's Junior" and inquired of the bounds of Roger Mathews.

Deposition of Nicholas Day, 5 August 1736, age about 48: At mouth of Polecat Creek about 15-16 years ago, he asked Edward Ward, and later asked John Taylor, about boundary.

Deposition of John Fuller, 5 August 1736, age about 56: On north side of Polecat Creek about 36 years ago, he lived with Robert Cutchin who said Col. Richardson told him the bounded tree of "Polecat."

Witnesses: Samuel Griffith, Roger Mathews, James Phillips and Nicholas Day and John Fuller.

59. Petition of Absolam Brown, 5 March 1736: In reference to part of "Hunting North" on east side of Bush River (James Phillips owned the other part). (Pages 249-252)

Commissioners appointed: Roger Mathews, Bennett Garrett, Henry Millam and Samuel Griffith.

Deposition of Antill Deaver, 3 May 1737, age about 52: About 25 years ago he lived with Col. James Phillips, deceased, and was told by Samuel Brown, Jr. which tree was the division tree between his father and Phillips.

Deposition of William Smith, 3 May 1737, age about 41: About 30 years ago he was with Samuel Brown, Sr. and was shown the bounded tree near Col. Phillips' boat house.

Deposition of Symond Peareson, 29 May 1737, age about 78: About 34 years ago Samuel Brown, Sr. (the father of the petitioner) showed him the bounded tree of land he bought from Collear; he swapped 100 acres of land with James Phillips.

60. Petition of Isaac Jackson, 5 June 1736: In reference to "Holmwood" in Gunpowder Neck near mouth of Gunpowder River near tract called "Sampson's Thickett" and a dispute over the dividing line. (pp. 253--end)

Commissioners appointed: Humphrey Wells Stokes, Henry Wetherall, Lemuel Howard and Richard Colegate.

Deposition of William Groves, August, 1736, age about 48:About 25 years ago he heard Col. James Maxwell and William Lenox speak of the bounds on east side of north branch of Gunpowder River and "Sampson's Thickett."

Deposition of Matthew Backer, August, 1736, age about 45: About 5 years ago James Maxwell, deceased (son of Colonel James Maxwell, deceased) was surveying his land. Deponent was chain carrier with John Dawney & they were shown the bounded tree of "Sampson's Thickett."

Deposition of John Dawney, August, 1736, age about 43: Gave a statement similar to Matthew Backer above.

Deposition of Aquilla Massey (Quaker), August, 1736, age about 33: His father, Jonathan Massey, showed James Maxwell, son of Col. James Maxwell, the bounds.

Deposition of John Hall, Sr., August, 1736, age about 79: On the east side of the north branch of the Gunpowder River, and on the south side of Watertown Creek, a little below dwelling house of Isaac Jackson, stood a beginning tree of "Holmwood" and the third bounded tree of "Mary's Bank."

1737-1762 (BOOK HWS & BB, NO. 4)

61. Petition of Edward Tully, August, 1736: In reference to a tract "The Hop Yard" on Jones Falls. (pp. 1-2)

Commissioners appointed 13 November 1736: John Risteau, Edward Stevenson, Nicholas Hale and Joseph Cromwell.

Deposition of Samuel Hooker (affirmator), 20 June 1737, age about 50: About 22 years ago Dutton Lane showed his father Thomas Hooker the boundary. Witness: Capt. John Boreing and George Barley.

62. Petition of Stephen Onion, March, 1736: In reference to part of "Samuel's Delight" at the mouth of the Little Falls of the Gunpowder River. (pp. 3-4)

Commissioners appointed 11 June 1737: Richard Cromwell, Humphrey Wells Stokes, Walter Tolley and Henry Wetherall.

Deposition of Robert Love (Quaker), 19 July 1737, age about 34: About 20 years ago John Bradshaw showed him the bounded tree.

Deposition of John Fuller, Sr., 19 July 1737, age about 56: About 30 years ago in the company of John Taylor and John Love, he was shown the bounded tree.

63. Petition of James Phillips, 1736: In reference to several tracts in St. George's Parish: "Chilbury," "Hunting North," "Chelsey," "Addition to Chilbury," "Batchelder's Addition," "Batchelder's Hope," "Crabhill," "Upper Eling," "Eaton," "James' Addition," "Pork Point," "Benjamin's Swap,"

"Lambeth Mash," "Covent Garden," "Mate's Angle," and "Water's Neck." (pp. 5-8)

Commissioners appointed 13 November 1736: Nathan Rigbie, Skipwith Cole, Edward Wakeman and William Bradford.

Deposition of John Hall, Esq., 30 May 1737, age about 80: About 30 years ago was in company of Col. James Phillips, father of James Phillips, and Samuel Brown. Col. Phillips showed him the bounded tree on Bush River.

Deposition of John Clark, 30 May 1737, age about 50: In 1716 he executed special warrant of resurvey for Col. James Phillips, deceased, on "James Park" adjoining "Chilbury."

Deposition of John Hall, Esq., 30 May 1737, age about 80: Was on "Butcher's Point" at mouth of middle creek of Bush River. On 4 December 1716, being surveyor, he surveyed the eastern branch of Bush River presently called Mill Branch.

Deposition of Roger Mathews, 30 May 1737, age about 52: About 18 years ago coming from house of David Thomas in January in company of Col. James Phillips, deceased father of present James Phillips, Col. Phillips purchased from the deponent the lands that the deponent had lately bought of Samuel & James Brown where Samuel Brown formerly lived.

Deposition of Richard Perkins, 20 June 1737, age about 50: About 30 years ago his father, Richard Perkins, showed him near a small branch of Susquehanna River, the beginning of a tract called "Jessop" and also "Eaton" belonging to Maj. James Phillips....and one "Haselwoof"....first taken up by Thomas Griffith. He was hog hunting with his father who told him that a tract called "Mt. Savall" belonged to Col. Henry Ward.

Deposition of William Simpson, 20 June 1737, age about 42: About 10 years ago James Smithers (late of Baltimore County, deceased) told him that he was the first man to build a house on a plantation south on Susquehanna River (by Aquila Paca, late of Baltimore County, deceased). He also knew the tree that parted the lands of Major James Phillips and Col. Henry Ward.

64. Petition of James Taylor, 1737: In reference to "Carter's Rest" formerly Samuel Jackson's part now in the petitioner's possession (and part in the possession of John Clark). (pp. 9-11)

Commissioners appointed 6 August 1737: Roger Mathews, John Hall, Jr., Parker Hall and Peregrine Frisby.

Deposition of Garrett Garetson, 20 October 1737, age not given: 50 years ago he lived with his grandfather --- Beetle who showed him where the trees stood in dividing the land between his grandfather and that of Robert Jones.

Deposition of John Jackson, 20 October 1737, age about 54: --- Morris served his time with Lodwick Martin, then part owner of "Carter's Rest." Morris told him about the apple trees between lands of Lodwick Martin and Edward Beetle.

65. Petition of William Carter, 4 March 1735: In reference to tract "Carter's Delight" near Jones Falls. (pp. 12-13)

Commissioners appointed 4 June 1736: Richard Gist, Charles Ridgely, William Rogers and Lloyd Harris.

Deposition of Thomas Green, 7 September 1737, age about 33 or 38: Seven years ago he was at John Carter's bound tree.

Deposition of Charles Gorsuch, 7 September 1737, age 50: Heard John Carter, John Cole, Jr., and others speak about the bounded tree.

66. Petition of Abraham Cord and Thomas Cord, 1735: In reference to "Cord's Purchase" part of "Musketo Proof." (pp. 14-15)

Commissioners appointed 6 March 1735: Edward Wakeman, Jervice (Jarvis) Gilbert, Henry Miller.
Deposition of John Hall, 3 November 1736, age about 80: The deponent transferred the said land to Thomas Cord, father of Abraham and Thomas Cord.

67. Petition of Isaac Webster, 1737: In reference to "Planter's Paradise" on north side of Deer Creek. (pp. 16-18)
Commissioners appointed 5 April 1737: Nathan Rigbie, Henry Cole, Skipwith Cole and Charles Worthington.
Deposition of Robert West, Sr., 13 September 1737, age about 68: About 35-36 years ago he was in company of Stephen Freeland who took up "Planter's Paradise" for Isaac Simmons.
Deposition of Gregory Farmer, Sr., 13 September 1737, age about 58: Gave statement similar to Robert West, Sr.
Deposition of Thomas Johnson, 13 September 1737, age about 80: About 20 years ago Isaac Simmons asked him about the bounds.

68. Petition of Joseph Taylor, 1737: In reference to tract called "Continuance" on Herring Run descending to Back River. (pp. 19-21)
Commissioners appointed 11 June 1737: Thomas Sheredine, John Risteau, Edward Stevenson and Lloyd Harris.
Deposition of John Wilmoth, 13 September 1737, age 54: About 12 years ago he was running line of "Taylor's Range" belonging to Richard Taylor and knows the ridge between the dwelling plantation of Joseph Taylor and Henry Stevenson.
Deposition of Luke Stansbury, 13 September 1737, age 43: About 12 years ago he was in company of Richard Taylor and John Hillen when shown the boundary.
Deposition of Walter James, 13 September 1737, age 43: About 12 years he was in company of Luke Stansbury and John Hillen when shown the boundary.
Deposition of Thomas Franklin, 13 September 1737, age 30: In 1734 he began the resurvey of "Continuance" for Joseph Taylor.
Deposition of William Parrish (Quaker), 13 September 1737, age 57: He was with his brother Edward Parrish and Richard Taylor when shown the boundary.

69. Petition of John Buck, Esq., merchant (Biddeford, Gr. Br.) 1737: In reference to a tract called "Pay My Debts" on Gwin's Falls near "Hunting Ridge." (pp. 22-24)
Commissioners appointed 5 August 1737: John Risteau, Christopher Gist, Nathaniel Gist and George Buchanan.
Deposition of Henry Butler, 1 September 1737, age about 69: About 30 years ago he was chain carrier when land was laid out.

70. Petition of Thomas Dimmitt, 10 July 1737: In reference to "Cole's Adventure" on Gwin's Run on north side of Jones Falls. pp. 25-26)
Commissioners appointed 11 June 1737: George Walker, Charles Ridgely, George Buchanan and John Gill.
Deposition of John Cole, Sr., 1 March 1737/8, age about 67: About 100 yards from Gwin's Run on east side was the beginning tree, about 20 feet south of boundary of John Parrish's land.
Deposition of Henry Butler, 1 March 1737/8, aged 60-70: About 50 or 60 yards east of present Garrison Road, near the Pimlico Swamp, is the boundary.

71. Petition of Joseph Taylor, 3 November 1737: In reference to a tract "Taylor's Range," originally called "Ill Will." (pp. 27-31)
    Commissioners appointed 22 December 1737: John Risteau, Lloyd Harris, Edward Stevenson and Thomas Sheredine.
    Deposition of Thomas Carr, 20 March 1737, age 59: About 23 years ago he was with Richard Taylor, deceased, when resurvey of "Taylor's Range" was made on west side of Herring Run.
    Deposition of Thomas Taylor, 20 March 1737, age 35: About 23 years ago with father Richard Taylor and John Isrell (Israel), "Ill Will" was surveyed by John Israel for Henry Roberts and boundary was the ridge between the dwelling plantation of Joseph Taylor and Henry Stevenson. About 20 years ago with father Richard Taylor and Edward Stevenson, deceased, he was shown the boundary. About 13 years ago with Richard Taylor, Luke Stansbury and John Hillen, he was shown the boundary between "Ill Will" and "Shoemaker's Hall."

72. Petition of Alexander Contee of Prince George's County, June, 1736: In reference to tract "Buck's Range" at the north east creek of Back River. (pp. 32-34)
    Commissioners appointed 5 June 1736: Thomas Sheredine, Richard Caswell, Luke Stansbury and Thomas Dulaney.
    Deposition of John Wilmoth, 29 July 1736, age 53: About 28-29 years ago he was shown the boundary of "Bucks Range" belonging to John Fanning.
    Deposition of John Boreing, 29 July 1726, age 53: About 12 years he was shown the boundary of "Bucks Range" that belonged to John Fanning.
    Deposition of John Harryman, 29 July 1736, age 42: About 5 years ago he was with Charles Smith when he was shown the boundary.

73. Petition of Lemuel Howard, 1738: In reference to "Andrew's Lott" at the head of Bush River. (pp. 35-36)
    Commissioners appointed 4 April 1738: Richard Caswell, Edward Day, Walter Tolley and Humphrey Wells Stokes.
    Deposition of Simon Pearson, 10 August 1738, age about 78: About 47-48 years ago Thomas Jones told him the boundary above the mouth of Bear Cabbin Branch near main branch of Bush River. He was with Capt. James Maxwell.

74. Petition of Thomas Gassaway, 1737: In reference to "Gassaway Ridge" in fork of Gunpowder River. (Note: All of the depositions refer to bounds of "Leaf's Chance," and "Gassaway Ridge" is not mentioned.) (pp 37-40)
    Commissioners appointed 11 March 1737: Richard Caswell, Edward Day, Walter Tolley and Humphrey Wells Stokes.
    Deposition of William Lowe 6 April 1738, age 51: About 24 years ago he was with John Taylor, then deputy surveyor of Baltimore County, who showed him the beginning tree of "Leaf's Chance" at corner of John Hutchins' land. About 14-15 years ago Col. John Dorsey was reversing a course of a tract called "Hangeing" and Nicholas Day came and showed him the boundary at the southwest corner of John Hutchins' plantation. Later, with Thomas Hutchins, an ancient man of the county (late deceased), deponent was shown the bounds.
    Deposition of John Hutchins, 28 April 1738, age about 40: His father Thomas Hutchins showed him the boundary near a creek running into great falls of Gunpowder River on the west side of John Hutchins' dwelling plantation now.
    Deposition of John Roberts alias Camble, 28 April 1738, age about 50: Boundary was on third branch of middle falls of Gunpowder River, he heard his father-in-law John Camble say.

Deposition of John Greer, Sr., 26 April 1738, age about 50: About 15 years ago John Taylor, former deputy surveyor of Baltimore County, showed him the boundary.

75. Petition of John Stoddert and Leonard Hollyday of Prince George's County, 1738: In reference to "Truman's Acquaintance" located in fork of the Gunpowder River. (pp. 41-43)
Commissioners appointed 4 August 1738: Richard Caswell, Humphrey Wells Stokes, Thomas Franklin & Thomas Gittings.
Deposition of John Greer, 30 November 1738, age 50: About 18 years ago he heard Charles Smith say Col. Richardson and Thomas Lightfoot came up the falls near the mouth of Long Green Run..... About a year or so later John Brooks of Calvert County and John Taylor came to his house.

76. Petition of William Wright, 1738: In reference to "Fuller's Outlett" on Middle River on Armstrong's Branch. (pp. 44-45)
Commissioners appointed 18 November 1738: Richard Caswell, William Bond, Luke Stansbury and Walter Tolley.
Deposition of Oliver Harrod, 26 February 1738, age 66: About 56 years ago he lived here on Armstrong's Creek.
Deposition of John Fuller, 26 February 1738, age about 57: About 33 years ago William Wright showed him the boundary. Said Wright has lived there for about 40 years.
Deposition of Samuel Watkins, 26 February 1738, age about 53: About 27 years ago William Wright (deceased about 15 years ago) told him the boundary.
Deposition of Jacob Wright, 26 February 1738, age 37: About 21 years ago his father, William Wright, told him the boundary.

77. Petition of William Bosley, 1738: In reference to "Bosley's Expectation" on south side of Bird River. (pp. 46-48)
Commissioners appointed 2 April 1739: Capt. William Bond, Edward Day, Walter Tolley and William Galloway.
Deposition of Oliver Harrod, 12 May 1739, age about 66: About 40 years ago he knew the beginning oak of "Arthur's Choice" and "Spring Neck," and Walter Bosley told him it was it was the beginning tree of his land....near Edward Thomas' dwelling plantation.
Deposition of John Greer, 12 May 1739, age about 50: About 40 years ago, uncle James Smithers showed him the bounded tree of "Arthur's Choice" about 40 yards from his father's dwelling house on south side of Bird River.

78. Petition of Richard Johns of Calvert County, 1738: In reference to "Mother's Care" on south side of south branch of Gunpowder River. (pp. 49-51)
Commissioners appointed 8 March 1738: William Bond, John Wilmott, Thomas Franklin and Darby Henly.
Deposition of Luke Stansbury, 20 July 1739, age about 50: In 1723 he and John Israel and Roger Mathews were appointed as Commissioners to determine bounds of "Mother's Care." They heard evidence from Thomas Dedman about the bounds of the tract, and about the plantation of William Towson on the south side of the branch flowing into the south branch of the Gunpowder River. Dutton Lane, surveyor, told them the bounds also.
Deposition of Thomas Franklin, 20 July 1739, age about 35: Last January 30th he was with Richard Johns, John Willmott, Sr., Thomas Dedman, and others. Thomas Dedman said that several years before he and Dutton Lane

were here, and Dutton Lane told him it was the beginning tree of his sister's land, "Mother's Care."

Deposition of John Willmott, 20 July 1739, age about 54: Last winter he and Richard Johns, Thomas Dedman, Thomas Franklin, and others were shown the bounds.

79. Petition of William Lynch, 1739: In reference to "Poplar Ridge" and "Jones Inheritance" in Patapsco Neck. (pp. 52-53)

Commissioners appointed 4 September 1739: Philip Jones, John Rattenburg, Robert North and Lloyd Harris.

Deposition of Capt. John Boreing, 25 February 1739, age about 57: About 38 years ago somebody told him the tree was beginning of land he (John Boreing) sold to Robuck Lynch which John Boreing's father bought from John Martaine....on branch of Bear Creek.

Deposition of Joseph Crouch, 25 February 1739, age about 48: He heard his wife, formerly wife of Robuck Lynch, speak of the boundary.

80. Petition of John Hall, 4 March 1739: In reference to "Hopewell's Marsh" in Gunpowder Neck. (pp. 54-56)

Commissioners appointed 8 March 1739: William Bradford, John Lloyd, William Dallam and Thomas Cole.

Deposition of William Groves, 1740, age about 50 (of St. John's Parish): He was with Richard Lennox and others 28 years ago and saw a tree close by Gunpowder River, and Richard Lennox said it was the beginning tree of his land ("Hopewell's Marsh").

Deposition of Mathew Beck, 1740, age about 50 (St. John's Parish): About 1732 he was with James Maxwell, deceased, John Dawney, Philip Jones (surveyor), and James Lennox at the bounded tree.

Deposition of John Dawney, 1740, age about 48 (St. John's Parish): Gave statement similar to M. Beck.

81. Petition of Samuel, Thomas and John Howard of Anne Arundel County, 1740, grandchildren of Philip Howard, and legatees of father Samuel Howard: In reference to tract "Howard's Range" surveyed in 1703 for Philip Howard (321 acres on branches of Deer Creek). (pp. 57-59)

Commissioners appointed 7 November 1740: William Bradford, John Paca, Benjamin Norris and Richard Ruff.

Deposition of Richard Rhoades, Sr., 5 February 1740, age about 57: About 35 years ago he was with Simon Pearson, late of Baltimore County, and John Howard (commonly called Lame John Howard) and was shown the boundary on the west side of Thomas Run.

Deposition of Isaac Butterworth, 5 February 1740, age about 37: About 14 years ago his father Isaac Butterworth (late of Baltimore County, dec'd) showed him the boundary.

Deposition of John Fuller, Sr., 5 February 1740, age about 61: About 35 years ago John Howard, Philip Howard, Andrew Wilply, Dutton Lane, Simon Pearson and the deponent were shown the boundary.

Deposition of Daniel Scott, Sr., 5 February 1740, age about 60: In May, 1700, John Howard, Philip Howard, Dutton Lane, Simon Pearson and the deponent were at the boundary between the mouth of Thomas Run and Deer Creek..."and John Howard killed a rattlesnake and took out its heart and swallowed it..."

Deposition of Hugh Copeland, Jr., 5 February 1740, age about 19: Last summer he went with Samuel Howard to Isaac Butterworth's house.

82. Petition of John Cole, Jr., 7 June 1737: In reference to "Daniel's Whimsey" near Jones Falls. (pp. 60-62)
  Commissioners appointed 6 August 1737: Lloyd Harris, Charles Ridgely, George Buchanan and William Fell.
  Deposition of John Cole, Sr., recorded in March, 1741, age about 67: About 30 years ago Capt. Thomas Roberts showed him the bounded tree of "Roberts' Park" and the beginning tree of "Daniel's Whimsey." About 20 years ago Nicholas Hale, Sr. showed him the boundary. He was also shown the bounds by John Christian.

83. Petition of Heathcoat Pickett, 1741: In reference to "Betty's Inheritance" on the falls of the Gunpowder River. (pp. 63-64)
  Commissioners appointed 21 November 1741: Thomas Cassaway, William Young, Richard Caswell and Edward Day.
  Deposition of John Roberts, 1 February 1741, age about 50: About 30 years ago he heard James Richardson speak of the bounds. The deponent and James Morrow kept "batchelders" house together and knew of the bounds.
  Deposition of Oliver Harrett, 1 February 1741, age about 68: About 30 years ago Charles Smith, James Richardson, and James Smithers told him the boundary.

84. Petition of George Eager, 1741: In reference to "Locust Lott" on Patapsco River. (pp. 65-67)
  Commissioners appointed 6 March 1741: George Buchanan, Robert North, William Rogers and William Fell.
  Deposition of William Parrish (Quaker), 24 May 1741, age about 63: He was shown the bounds by Moses Edwards and Richard Gist in order to find "Talbot's Plains" now called "Mary's Plains." Dr. George Walker's brick house was also mentioned.

85. Petition of Mathew Coulter, 1742: In reference to "Brother's Choice" on west side of north west branch of Patapsco River. (pp. 68-69)
  Commissioners appointed 6 August 1742: John Pisteau, William Fell, Josephus Murray and Nathaniel Gist.
  Deposition of Henry Butler, 21 September 1742, age about 74: About 20 years go Edward Roberts, Richard Gist, Thomas Cromwell, Sr., William Cromwell, Sr., and Nathan Brothers showed him the bounds.

86. Petition of William Fell, 1742: In reference to tract called "Carter's Delight."(pp. 70-72)
  Commissioners appointed 10 November 1742: Captain Thomas Sheredine, Captain Robert North, Charles Gorsuch and John Ensor.
  Deposition of Thomas Green, 10 February 1742, age about 37: About 14 years ago John Carter, late of Baltimore County, showed him the bounds near old main road and in line of land called "Mountenays."
  Deposition of Charles Gorsuch, 10 February 1742, age about 57: John Carter showed him the boundary.
  Deposition of William Carter, 10 February 1742, age about 26: His father, John Carter, showed him the boundary.

87. Petition of Joseph Thomas, 1742: In reference to tract called "James Forecast" and "Horn's Point" on the side of Salt Pater Creek. (pp. 73-76)
  Commissioners appointed 10 December 1742: Richard Caswell, George Presbury, Bart. Milhuse and William Bond.

Deposition of Oliver Harrett, planter, 31 January 1742, age about 69: About 50 years ago he lived with Thomas James who owned "Horn Point." About 40 years ago he was shown "James Forecast" and John Rockhold's land boundary.
Deposition of John Rockhold, planter, 31 January 1742, age about 31: About 12 years he was with his father Charles Rockhold and was shown the bounds.

88. Petition of Charles Carroll, Esq., 1743: In reference to 600 acre tract called "Thompson's Lott" on south side of south branch of the Gunpowder River. (pp. 77-79)
Commissioners appointed 10 June 1743: William Young, Thomas Gassaway, Walter Tolley and Stephen Onion.
Deposition of John Greer, 25 July 1743, age about 55: About 30 years ago John Taylor, who then lived on south side of Gunpowder River near the ferry and afterwards went to Carolina and if living would be about 78 years old, showed him the bounds, and the second tree of tract called "Adventure Addition."

89. Petition of Charles Ridgely, 1742: In reference to "Rich Neck" on middle branch of Patapsco River. (pp. 80-83)
Commissioners appointed 6 August 1742: Thomas Sheredine, George Buchanan, William Hammond and Robert North.
Deposition of William Parish (Quaker), 14 March 1742, age 60: About 30 years ago John Gill, deceased, lived on land called "Black Walnut" adjoining "Rich Neck."
Deposition of John Parish, Jr. (Quaker), 14 March 1742, age 40: About 25 years ago he was shown the bounds.
Deposition of William Hamilton, 14 March 1742, age 60: About 34-36 years ago John Gill showed him a tree and said it was his bounded tree.
Deposition of William Wells, 14 March 1742, age 35: When he was a boy, Darby ---- , deceased, told him about the bounds, and Edward Parish, deceased, ran a dividing line between him and Gill's land.
Deposition of Edward Parish, 14 March 1742, age 36: About 20 years ago when line of "Rich Neck" was run, there was a dispute between his father (John Parish) and John Gill over the boundary.
Deposition of John Arnold, 14 March 1742, age 33: About 19 years ago Jane Gill, deceased, told him of the bounds.

90. Petition of George Presbury, 1743: In reference to "Surveyor's Point" on south side of Gunpowder River. (pp. 84-85)
Commissioners appointed 10 June 1743: Capt. Richard Caswell, Capt. William Bond, Daniel Scott, and William Andrews.
Deposition of James Isham, 21 July 1743, age about 75: About 43 years ago he lived on this plantation.
Deposition of Benjamin Legoe, 21 July 1743, age about 69: About 40 years ago he lived on Goldsmith's land, near Presbury, and heard John Anderson say Goldsmith's land ("Collett") joined with Harwood's land.
Deposition of Charles Pines, 21 July 1743, age about 36: He heard old standers (?) say George Presbury's land joined Harwood's and they didn't know when Anthony Asher would find his, and the spring branch marsh 20 years ago just appeared to be a valley.
Deposition of James Presbury, gentleman, 21 July 1743, age about 59: About 35 years ago he was informed by John Hall, Esq., late of Baltimore

County, deceased, that he knew the bounds. He lived on this plantation 10 years.

91. Petition of Benjamin Colegate, 1743: In reference to "Huntingtown" on north side of Patapsco River and west side of Balls Creek. (pp. 87-89)
Commissioners appointed 5 August 1743: William Rogers, Sabret Sollers, Charles Gorsuch and Robert North.
Deposition of John Talbot, age about 37: About 16-18 years ago John Gorsuch told him his (John Gorsuch's) father showed him the bounds.
Deposition of John Colegate, age about 35: He came here with John Powell and John Gorsuch showed him John Powell's bounded tree.

90. Petition of Richard Kimble, 1743: In reference to "Expactation." John Watkins cut down a bounded tree of "New Park" now in possession of James Garrison and adjoining the petitioner's land. (pp. 90-93)
Commissioners appointed 9 March 1743: Peregrine Frisby, James Phillips, John Mathews and John Hall of Cranberry.
Deposition of George Eves, 19 October 1744, age about 75: About 27-28 years ago he was with Samuel Jackson and was shown the bounds, and a year or two later Peter Lester showed him the bounded tree of Ivo's land.
Deposition of Thomas Burchfield (of Adam), 19 October 1744 age about 32: John Watkins ordered him to cut down tree.
Deposition of Edward Cantwell, 19 October 1744, age about 45: About 12 years ago he was where John Watkins had cleared the land.
Deposition of Col. John Hall, 19 October 1744, age about 43: About 16 years ago he served on Commission to perpetuate the bounds of "New Park."
Deposition of John Clark, 19 October 1744, age about 60: He served on Commission with John Hall and took deposition of Martin Depost and Thomas Burchfield about the boundary.
Deposition of John Jackson, Sr., 19 October 1744, age about 60: He was with Owen Sullavant and shown boundary.
Commission set up bounds on south side of main road near bridge called the Chinkerpin Bridge.

93. Petition of Aquila Paca, 1742: In reference to "Delph" and "Delph's Neglect." (pp. 94-97)
Commissioners appointed 5 June 1742: Thomas White, Edward Wakeman, George Lester and Samuel Griffin.
Deposition of Thomas Williamson, 24 March 1743, age about 50: About 21 years ago he was with Thomas Newsom with whom he lived and Thomas Newsom told him about the bounds.
Deposition of James Rutter, 24 March 1743, age about 55: About 14 years ago he was with William Smith who told him about the bounds, and sometime after he was with George Murray who told him about the bounds. John Crockett told George Murray about the bounds on west side of Delph Creek near its mouth.
Witnesses: John Baley and Major John Hall.

94. Petition of William Young, 1743: In reference to "Sewell's Fancy" in fork of Gunpowder River. (pp. 98-101)
Commissioners appointed 1 December 1743: Thomas Sheredine, Stephen Onion, Nicholas Ruxton Moore and Talbot Risteau.
Deposition of Major Thomas Sheredine, 14 June 1744, age about 45: 7 years ago he was with Nicholas Day and some others and ran out "Sewell's Fancy" bounds on south east side of Walter Perdue's house and plantation

where he now dwells. Nicholas Day said tree was second bounded tree of "Sewell's Fancy" & beginning tree of "Thompson's Choice."

Deposition of Capt. John Smith (Calvert Co.) 14 June 1744: age about 25: About 7 years ago he was with Thomas Sheredine, Nicholas Day and others and was shown the bounds.

Deposition of Walter Purdue, 14 June 1744, age about 62: About 7 years ago he was with Thomas Sheredine, Nicholas Day, John Smith & William Young and was shown the bounds.

95. Petition of Thomas Sligh, 1744: In reference to "Wells Angles" on Back River. (pp. 102-105)

Commissioners appointed 8 June 1744: Thomas Sheredine, Tobias Stansbury, Patrick Lynch and William Lynch.

Deposition of Henry Oyston, 1 September 1744, age about 40: About 16 years ago Nicholas Gorstwick showed him the bounds.

Deposition of Isaac Sampson, 1 September 1744, age 71: About 50 years ago Rowland Thornbury showed him bounds on a point beside Back River as well as Adam's land called "Welcome" and the beginning tree of a 41 acre tract called "Goose Harbour" he had taken up. The oak by main road near head of Bread and Cheese Creek on west side is not bounded tree of any tract, but John Poyston bound it without any authority to hinder anyone from taking up the land.

Deposition of Henry Oyston, 1 September 1744: Sixteen years ago he was with Isaac Sampson and shown the boundary and John Bowen showed him the bounds and he believed that "Welcome" was escheated.

96. Petition of John Wooden, 1744: In reference to 570 acre tract, part of "Parishes Range." (pp. 106-109)

Commissioners appointed 6 December 1744: George Buchanan, Charles Ridgely, Alexander Lawson and Robert North.

Deposition of William Parish (Quaker), 15 March 1744, age about 60: He was brought to a dead red oak lying in woods within one quarter mile of Richard Demitts house and to southwest of said house near which stands a poplar tree; oak is bounded tree and the dividing tree between Mathew Hawkins and John Wooden, said lands being part of tract "Parishes Range." Deponent has known tree 30-40 years and was shown it by brother Edward; white oak on a draught of Gwins Run is dividing tree between lands of George Ogg and John Wooden, part of "Parishes Range," now in possession of John Wooden, known 30 years; white oak near head of a draught of Seader Run is corner tree of George Ogg's land, part of "Parishes Range" now in possession of John Wooden.

About 30 years ago old Edward Parish, old George Ogg, old John Wooden and Dutton Lane (surveyor) were shown the land bounds. About 34 years ago the woods being on fire George Ogg pointed out the bounded tree, said tree was on land he lived on, part of "Parishes Range," and grown near John Parish's plantation and near the main road.

97. Petition of John Edwards, 1744: In reference to "Edwards Lott" and "Hicksons." (pp. 110-111)

Commissioners appointed 8 March 1744: Thomas Sheredine, Robert North, William Fell and John Insor.

Deposition of Nicholas Haile, 10 June 1745, age about 41: About 30 years ago with father, Nicholas Haile, deponent was shown the bounded tree of "Hail's Addition" and also of Moses Edwards land.

Deposition of John Merryman, 10 June 1745, age about 67: He was involved in the land survey for Moses Edwards.

Deposition of Thomas Butler, 10 June 1745, age about 63: About 20 years ago Jonathan Hanson, late of Baltimore County, deceased, showed him the tree on north side of path leading from deponent's plantation to plantation where Jonathan Hanson now lives, and also shown bounded tree of Hickson's land.

98. Petition of Edward Day, 1744: In reference to "Taylor's Mount" and "Dixon's Chance." (pp. 112-115)

Commissioners appointed 6 December 1744: Richard Caswell, William Young, William Bond and George Presbury.

Deposition of Major Thomas Sheredine, 4 October 1745, age about 46: In 1729 (when Sheriff) he and Philip Jones, Jr. (surveyor) were on Commission to perpetuate the bounds of "Taylor's Mount" and "Dixon's Chance," and the depositions from John Greer, James Smithers (Smithen) and John Hall as filed by Col. Richardson spoke of the bounds near house that Mr. Hutcheson now lives in.

Deposition of Oliver Barriott, 4 October 1745, age about 70: About 46 years ago James Smithers (Smithen) told him the bounds of Col. Richardson's land, and he was also told the bounds by John Greer, Lawrence Richardson, and James Richardson, son of Col. Richardson.

99. Petition of Robert Dutton, 1745: In reference to "Hogg Point."

Commissioners appointed 5 November 1745: Richard Caswell, William Young, Walter Tolley and William Savory. (pp. 116-117)

Deposition of Dianah Jones, 25 December 1745, age about 46: About 24 years ago her deceased husband Benjamin showed her the tree on Gunpowder River as the dividing tree of "Hogg Point" and "Merrikan's Inheritance."

Deposition of Hesther Camaran, 25 December 1745, age about 33: About 11 years ago one came with her husband John, (deceased) to live on "Hogg Point."

100. Petition of Gabriel Parker, 1745: In reference to "Tapley Neck" between Gunpowder River and Bush River. (pp. 118-120)

Commissioners appointed 6 August 1745: William Dallam, William Young, Nathan Richardson and William Savory.

Deposition of John Debrular, 15 March 1745, age about 73. About 9-10 years ago Gilbert Crockett showed him bounded tree of "Tapley Neck" and "Locust Neck."

101. Petition of George Plater, Esq., 1745: In reference to "Taskers Camp" in fork of Gunpowder River. (pp. 121-122)

Commissioners appointed 5 November 1745: William Young, Richard Caswell, William Dallam and Thomas Gittings.

Deposition of Thomas Gudgeon, 15 March 1745, age about 67: About 48-49 years ago he helped carry chain when Colonel Richardson surveyed "Taskers Camp."

Deposition of John Fuller, 15 March 1745, age about 68: About 20 years go Thomas Gudgeon told him same as above.

102. Petition of Benjamin Bowen on behalf of Josias Bowen, 1745: In reference to "Kinderton" on Patapsco River. (pp. 123-124)

Commissioners appointed 5 November 1745: Thomas Sheredine, Robert North, Philip Jones, Jr. and William Lynch.

Deposition of Thomas Franklin, 4 February 1745, age about 40: In 1738 he was with John Gardner who showed him the beginning tree of "Gardner's Addition."

103. Petition of William Lynch, 1746: In reference to 100 acres which John Boreing formerly purchased from John Martain. (pp. 125-128)
Commissioners appointed 6 June 1746: Philip Jones, Sabrit Sollers, William McCubbin and Capt.Tobias Stansbury, Jr.
Deposition of Capt. John Boreing, 20 April 174?, age about 62: About 50 years, riding down the main road of Patapsco Neck behind father-in-law John Ferry for his overseer, Thomas Clinik told him of the bounds and that he had sold land called "Poplar Ridge" to Robuck Lynch.
Deposition of Tobias Stansbury, 20 April 174?, age about 56: About 30 years ago he was clearing land with Samuel Arding and shown land known as "Deep Valley" on Walton's Creek of Back River.
Deposition of Patrick Lynch, 20 April 174?, age about 47: His mother and his father told him that this was the land that his father bought from John Boreing.

104. Petition of Robert North, 1746: In reference to "Limes Pitts" on drafts of Jones Falls. (pp. 129-132)
Commissioners appointed 8 August 1746: Samuel Owings, Capt. Henry Morgan, Capt. John Cockey and Christ. Randall (Christopher Randall).
Deposition of Violet Gist, 12 December 1746, age about 30: John Cole showed her the bounded tree of "Cole's Caves."
Deposition of Thomas Gist, 12 December 1746, age about 33: His father, Richard Gist, said John Cole showed him the bounds of "Cole's Caves."
Deposition of Edward Choate, 12 December 1746, age about 60: Richard Gist said that John Cole showed him "Cole's Caves." John Cole told him at the request of Dr. Carroll.
Deposition of Cornelius Howard, 12 December 1746, age about 39: About 12-14 years ago when a Commissioner for Dr. Carroll proved bounds of "Cole's Caves" he heard John Cole speak of the bounds.
Deposition of Josephus Murray (Quaker), 12 December 1746, age about 58: With Richard Gist and William Hamilton who was then magistrate, the deponent heard John Cole swear before the magistrate regarding the bounds of "Cole's Caves."

105. Petition of James Moore, 18 June 1747: In reference to "The Proprietary's Manor." (Commissioners not named) (p. 133)
Deposition of Thomas Gittings, 1747, age about 66: About 5-6 years ago with James Moore, John Holloway and John Chamberland he was shown the bounds.
Deposition of Jeremiah Cook, 1747, age about 38: About 4 years ago last March while with Edward Cox (son of Edward) he was shown the bounds.

106. Petition of James Phillips, 1746: In reference to "Benjamin's Choice" and "Hylands." (pp. 134-136)
Commissioners appointed 8 August 1746: Parker Hall, John Mathews, Daniel Ruff and James Osborn.
Deposition of John Cleark (Clark), 29 November 1746, age 60: On 24 December 1746 he was acting as special witness for James Phillips, gentleman, on "James Park" boundary.
Deposition of Parker Hall, 29 November 1746, age about 40: About 16-17 years ago with father John Hall, Thomas White, and others, Esquire Hall told

them bounds of a tract Col. Phillips bought from Francis Holland called
"Benjamin's Choice" at edge of Cranberry Swamp.

Deposition of John Atkinson, 29 November 1746, age about 55: About 16-17
years ago with Esquire Hall, Thomas White and others, Esquire Hall told them
of the tract bought by Col. Phillips from Francis Holland, called
"Benjamin's Choice."

107. Petition of William Young, 1746: In reference to tract "Sewell's
Fancy." (pp. 137-139)

Commissioners appointed 4 November 1746: Charles Ridgley, John Paca,
Thomas Sheredine and William Dallam.

Deposition of Robert Brown (Anne Arundel County) 15 April 1747, age about
63: About 28-29 years ago he came to Richard Lenoxes in Baltimore County
intending to purchase part of tract called "Hill's Forrest" in the fork of
the Gunpowder River from Joseph Hill, who advised him to call on Richard
Lenox and Charles Simmons to show him the land called "Hill's Forrest" and a
bounded tree of the land of Major Sewell, and beginning tree of "Thompson's
Choice."

Deposition of Thomas Sheredine, 15 April 1747, age about 48: About 10
years ago William Young asked him to run out a tract of land called
"Sewell's Fancy" in the fork of the Gunpowder River. Nicholas Day took him
to a small stony ridge on the south east side of the house and plantation
where Walter Purdue (Perdue) lived to show him the bounded trees of
"Sewell's Fancy" and "Thompson's Choice."

108. Petition of Charles Ridgely, 7 August 1746: In reference to three
tracts on south side of great falls of Gunpowder River called "Northamton,"
"Thomas Park," and "Hampton Court." Also, to examine the bounds of a tract
called "Raven's Refuge" partly in possession of Solomon Hillen. (pp.
140-146)

Commissioners appointed 8 August 1746: William Hammond, Thomas Franklin,
Samuel Owings and Edward Stevenson.

Deposition of Tobias Stansbury, Sr., 8 December 1746, age about 60: He was
with his uncle, Luke Raven, when he had "Raven's Refuge" surveyed by James
Crook on Petersons Run. A white oak, one of the boundaries, was on a ridge
by a path leading from dwelling plantation of John Willmott Sr. to plantation where Thomas Boreing lately lived and now the plantation of John
Boreing. The two plantations are on the west side of a small run or branch
which falls into Peterson Run.

Deposition of John Willmott, Sr., 8 December 1746, age about 67: About 30
years ago he was riding with Captain Thomas Roberts on north side of Richard
Cole's plantation when he was shown the bounded tree of Darnall's land
called "Northamton," commonly called Peterson's land.

Deposition of John Boreing, Sr., 8 December 1746, age about 64: About 27
years ago he was with Thomas Towson (late of Baltimore County, deceased) on
south side of the great falls of Gunpowder River (at top of a round hill)
and was shown the bounded tree of land called Peterson's or "Northampton"
and shown where William Towson's plantation is now. He was also told by
Henry Stone, or John Wheeler, bounds on Setter Hill Run, a draft of
Gunpowder Falls.

109. Petition of Alexander Lawson and Company, 1747: In reference to "Back
Lingon" lying on Back Gunpowder or Bird River. (pp. 146-148)

Commissioners appointed 3 June 1747: William Bond, Walter Tolley, Talbot
Risteau and George Presbury.

Deposition of John Greer, 8 August 1747, age about 58: He was told by his uncle, --- Smithers, or his father-in-law, Lawrence Richardson, that a Spanish oak was the beginning tree of the land called "Back Lingon" and it was about 45 years ago when he first saw it opposite the plantation where Capt. Richard Caswell lately lived.

110. Petition of Michael Macnemarra of Annapolis, 1747: In reference to tract "Pimlico" ("Pimbleco"?) (pp. 149-151)
Commissioners appointed 3 March 1747: Dr. George Buchanan, Samuel Owings, Joseph Cromwell and Charles Ridgely.
Deposition of John Price, 13 August 1747, age about 57: Property is east of Garrison Road and at back of Henry Butler's "New Design." Henry Butler died within the last two years.
Deposition of Haman (Amon) Butler, 13 August 1747, age about 23: His father, Henry Butler, told him the bounds.

111. Petition of William Hammond and Oliver Cromwell, 1746: In reference to "Cromwell's Chance." (pp. 152-156)
Commissioners appointed 10 March 1746: Dr. George Buchanan, Capt. Charles Ridgely, Capt. Darby Lux, Capt. Robert North.
Deposition of Daniel Rawlings (Quaker) 8 May 1747, age 52: In 1738 he was called with Henry Butler at the request of William Hammond and Oliver Cromwell to carry chains to survey "Cromwell's Chance." Henry Butler showed deponent the first tree of "Cromwell's Chance" and the beginning tree of "Galleypott Levell."
Deposition of Christopher Randall, 8 May 1747, age 38: About 9 years ago Henry Butler showed him the bounds.
Deposition of John Price, 8 May 1747, age 56: Henry Butler showed him the bounds and run called Cromwell's Run.
Deposition of Amon Butler, 8 May 1747, age 24: His father, Henry Butler, showed him the land (and mentions "Galley").
Deposition of James Gardiner, 8 May 1747, age 42: Henry Butler showed him the bounds and the beginning tree of Rattenberry's land.

112. Petition of Samuel and Elizabeth Smith, 1744 or 1747: In reference to tract called "East Humphrys." (pp. 157-161)
Commissioners appointed 6 August 1747: Thomas Sheredine, Charles Ridgely, Sabrit Sollers and Thomas Franklin.
Deposition of John Sergant, 25 February 1747, age 40: About 20 years ago Jonas Robinson was at the mouth of Clapper's Creek and showed him the bounded tree of Capt. Joseph Merryman's land.
Deposition of Merryman Cox, 25 February 1747, age about 25: About 9-10 years ago he was with his grandmother, Mary Merryman, who showed him the land which his grandfather Charles Merryman's widow called "East Humphry," where his grandfather Charles Merryman lived and planted a boundary tree in presence of four neighbors: Jonas Robinson, Jonathan Plowman, John Rawlings and John Sing.
Deposition of Abraham Eagleston, 25 February 1747, age about 37: Land at mouth of a cove on the east side of the mouth of Clappers Creek to be run out by Tobias Stansbury. Samuel Smith showed him a cherry tree boundary of Mr. Merryman.
Deposition of Tobias Stansbury, 25 February 1747, age about 60: Was told by Jonas Robinson that Capt. Merryman showed him how to survey land called "Cuckold's Hall" that laid by said land.

ABSTRACTS OF BALTIMORE COUNTY LAND COMMISSIONS

Deposition of John Merryman, 25 February 1747, age about 70: When he was about 10 years old the tree opposite the mouth of Powell's Creek on west side of Clapper's Creek was shown to him by his father, Charles Merryman.

Deposition of Samuel Merryman, 25 February 1747, age about 65: When he was a small boy he was shown the tree stated in John Merryman's deposition, and said the tree was the dividing line between him and Nicholas Fitzsimonds.

Deposition of Patrick Lynch, 25 February 1747, age about 48: About 10-12 years ago he was standing with Benjamin Bowen, late of Baltimore County, deceased, and Captain Robert North at a bounded tree at the side of a point called "The Mountain" and westward of the plantation of Capt. North. Benjamin Bowen showed him the boundary tree of his lands and Capt. Merryman's lands and Capt. North's lands. About 20 years ago Jonas Bowen, late of Baltimore County, deceased, showed him the bounded tree of Captain Charles Merryman's land.

113. Petition of Col. Thomas White, 1747: In reference to "North Yarmouth" at head of Swan Creek. (pp. 162-164)
Commissioners appointed 27 November 1747: Winstone Smith, Richard Johns, John Mathews and James Phillips.
Deposition of Thomas Mitchell, 22 February 1747, age about 65: Many years ago George Morgan (now deceased) told him the bounds of land called "Dillingsgate." Also mentioned Frances Whitehead.
Deposition of John Clark, 22 February 1747, age about 62: Stated that the second tree of "Hammond's Hope" is the second tree of "North Yarmouth."

114. Petition of William Barney, 1747: In reference to part of "Morgan's Delight." (pp. 165-169)
Commissioners appointed 4 March 1747: William Hammond, Capt. Robert North, Capt. Henry Morgan, and Joseph Taylor (Quaker).
Deposition of Samuel Hooker (Quaker), 27 May 1748, age about 62: Has known bounded tree for about 47 years. His father Thomas Hooker and Dutton Lane (both deceased) told him they were present when tree was bound for second tree of "Friend's Discovery" and beginning tree of "Morgan's Delight." About 44 years ago Durton Lane showed him the second tree of "Morgan's Delight." About 34 years ago his father Thomas Hooker and Morgan Murray, deceased, showed him the third tree of this tract, and also showed him the third tree of Job Evans' "Friend's Discovery."
Deposition of Joseph Murray, 27 May 1748, age about 31: About 12 years ago he was with his father Morgan Murray and his uncle Jabez Murray and others, and his father showed him the bounded tree of "Morgan's Delight" and "Friendship's Discovery" and the beginning tree of William Barney's part of "Morgan's Delight." He was present when uncle Josephus Murray swore to tree about 17 years ago and his father and William Barney, deceased, were also there.
Deposition of Capt. Greenbury Dorsey, 27 May 1748, age about 37: Last March he was proposing purchasing "Morgan's Delight" from William Barney and William Barney told him the bounds.
Deposition of Joab (Job) Evans, 27 May 1748, age about 43: About 16 years ago he was with Morgan Murray, deceased, who showed him the beginning tree of tract called "Jabrez Gillard."

115. Petition of John Bailey, 1747: In reference to "Contrivance" near head of Delph Creek and in possession of Nathaniel Smith. (pp. 165-173)
Commissioners appointed 27 November 1747: James Phillips, John Mathews, Daniel Ruff and James Osbourne.

Deposition of John Jackson Sr., 21 October 1748, age about 65: About 15-16 years ago he worked for William Smith who told him which tree was the beginning tree of his land.

Deposition of James Moore, 2 May 1748, age about 67: Third bounded tree of "His Lordship's Manor" was shown to him by John Fuller as told by Edward Cox. Archibald Rollo, late of Baltimore County, deceased, told him John Crockett said this was the bounded tree.

116. Petition of Rev. Hugh Carlile, Rector, St.George's Parish: In reference to "Rayley" and "Matson's Lott." (pp. 174-176)

Commissioners appointed 3 March 1746: William Bradford, Jacob Lusby, Daniel Maccomas and John Paca.

Deposition of Abraham Cord, 29 April 1747, age about 46: About 17-18 years ago William Cook showed him the bounded tree of Glebe land, formerly land of Francis Holland of Swan Creek; land formerly belonged to Parson Yoe.

Deposition of John Clark, 29 April 1747, age about 60: In 1716-1717 at request of Francis Holland, who was then in possession of "Rayley" and "Matson's Lott," he was shown the bounds. In 1719 William Cook told him about the bound tree of "Rob" and the beginning tree of "Hazard."

117. Petition of Charles Carroll of Annapolis, 1749: In reference to tracts "Elio Carroll" ("Ely O Carroll") and "Letter Luna." (pp. 177-180)

Commissioners appointed 8 November 1749: Charles Ridgely, George Ashmon (Quaker), Nicholas Orrick & Daniel Rawlings.

Deposition of Josephus Murray (Quaker), 12 February 1749, age about 61: He was shown the land to be near Talbot's Great Horse Pasture Branch on east side near mouth of the branch where it emptied into Jones Falls. About 2-3 years before Piercey Welsh died, he showed the deponent the beginning tree of "Ely O Carroll." Some years later the deponent came with Richard Gist and he said the same tree was the beginning tree of "Ely O Carroll."

Deposition of Edward Tulley, 12 February 1749, age about 62: He said as he and Percey Welsh were riding between the "Garrison Quarter" and William Talbot's, Welsh pointed to Horse Pasture Branch and said Charles Carroll's land was down that branch. The deponent said about 30 years ago he and Piercey Welsh noticed the original boundary tree was decaying and they bound a tree nearby to replace it.

118. Petition of Elizabeth Mathews (relict of Roger Mathews), 6 December 1742: In reference to "Edward's Lott" that formerly belonged to Dr. George Buchanan, and "Pearson's Park" that was originally surveyed for Simon Pearson, now deceased. Both tracts on or near Binam's (Bynum's) Run. (pp. 181-184)

Commissioners appointed 10 December 1742: Parker Hall, Aquila Paca, William Bradford and John Paca.

Deposition of Robert Collings, 12 September 1747, age about 40: About 16-18 years ago Michael James took up 50 acres and got Simon Pearson to show it to him. Deponent went with them to help carry chain. Michael James and John Tyle (Tyll) showed him boundary tree of "Pearson's Park." About 12-13 years ago the deponent was overseer for Roger Mathews and heard Richard Rhodes was going to take up land near said quarter but Simon Pearson told him there was no vacant land worthwhile.

Deposition of Roger Donohue, 12 September 1747, age about 36: About 7 years ago Col. Thomas White had him bring Daniel Scott to the beginning tree of "South Hampton" that stood by a branch close to Mr. Mathews' quarter.

Deposition of Richard Rhodes, 12 September 1747, age about 63: About 23 years ago Simon Pearson showed him bounded tree and said it was bounded by Thomas Shard. About 27 years ago Daniel Scott was with him on Binam's (Bynum's) Run and said it was the boundary tree of "Pearson's Park."

119. Petitioner's Name Not Given, Nor Date, Nor Commissioners With Respect to the Following Deposition (p. 185):

Deposition of William Cox (miller), 10 December 1745: While living at plantation and mill formerly in possession of Robert West, Jr. known as "West's Mill" on draught of Deer Creek, a laboring man named Thomas Garrett was hired. On 29 November 1745 Garrett cut down the boundary tree of "West's Beginning" now owned by William Cox. Cox has set up a bounded stone near the stump of the original tree in presence of Robert West, Sr., Robert Hawkins, Sr., Gregory Farmer, Sr., Daniel Murdaugh, Robert West, Jr.

120. Petition of Samuel Budd, 2 June 1747: In reference to "Wisk" (alias "Danby") and "Dickenson" adjoining on north side of Back River on Back River Neck. (pp. 186-190)

Commissioners appointed 3 June 1747: Thomas Franklin, Walter Dallas, Phillip Jones and Thomas Hynes.

Deposition of Philip Jones, 23 July 1750, age about 49: Some years ago while resurveying "Double Trouble" for Robert Robertson in Back River Neck he saw the beginning tree of Esq. Samuel Young of Anne Arundel County on north side of Back River above Chancellor's Point.

Deposition of John Long, 23 July 1750, age about 39: About 17-18 years ago he was with his aunt Jane Knight and was shown the beginning tree of Col. Samuel Young's land, and later with Luke Stansbury now deceased, saw the same tree.

Deposition of William Lynch, 23 July 1750, age about 43: About 11-12 years ago he was with Edward Fotrell, Luke Stansbury, Alexander Lawson, John Mahone and William Hoppman. The last two were to show Edward Fotrell the beginning of the land lately belonging to Col. Samuel Young but then in possession of Fotrell. Someone in the group ran a line down the river toward Thomas Stansbury's plantation.

Deposition of Walter Dallas, 23 July 1750, age about 46: In 1746 Thomas Stansbury obtained commission to prove the bounds of "Dickenson." Thomas Franklin, Solomon Hellin and the deponent took depositions on 30 August 1746 from John Willmott, Sr. and Christopher Dukes, Sr. Willmott, then about 66 years old, said about 25-26 years ago he ran out the tract of land where Thomas Stansbury lives. He and Stansbury, along with John Rogers, came to Sawpit Point where the boundary of "Dickenson" begins. Christopher Dukes, then aged about 55 years, said about 35-36 years ago John Hayes asked him to go with him to run out Thomas Stansbury's land.

Deposition of Thomas Franklin, 23 July 1750, age about 44: In 1746 he was appointed Commissioner along with Walter Dallas and Solomon Hellin to take depositions of John Willmott, Sr. and Christopher Dukes, Sr. regarding bounds of Thomas Stansbury's land "Dickenson." They met at Sawpit Point on the north side of Back River, a little below John Long's plantation.

121. Petition of Thomas Bond, 1750: In reference to "Bedford Resurveyed." (pp. 191-193)

Commissioners appointed 21 November 1750: Samuel Owings, Christopher Randall, Joseph Cromwell and Cornelius Howard.

Deposition of Cornelius Howard, 17 January 1750, age about 42: About 18-19 years ago Philip Jones was resurveying "Bedford" for Mathew Coulter.

Deponent heard John Sinkins, now deceased, identify the bounded tree of "Mount Organ."

Deposition of Charles Hissey, 17 January 1750, age about 48: Was with John Sinkins, deceased, who showed him the boundary tree of "Bedford Resurveyed."

Deposition of Mathew Coulter, 17 January 1750, age about 70: When he was having "Bedford" resurveyed he saw the boundary tree.

Deposition of John Sinkins, 17 January 1750, age about 27: About 15-16 years ago he saw beginning tree of "Bedford."

Deposition of Mathew Coulter, 17 January 1750, age about 70: He knows of the beginning tree of "Bedford" and "Logston's Addition Resurveyed."

Deposition of Charles Hissey, 17 January 1750, age about 48: He knows of the beginning tree of "Bedford."

122. Petition of William Hammond, 1750: In reference to "Cole's Addition." (pp. 194-197)

Commissioners appointed 7 June 1750: Darby Lux, John Ridgely, William Rogers and Joshua Hall.

Deposition of Thomas Sheredine, 6 August 1750: About 15-20 years ago John Cole, late of Baltimore County, deceased, at request of William Green showed the boundary tree at the lower end of Green's plantation. John Cole sold "Cole's Choice" where Charles Gorsuch lived to Richard Owings, merchant in Baltimore County.

Deposition of John Ensor, Sr., 6 August 1750, age about 55: About 18 years he and his father-in-law John Cole were on the west side of Mountanys Run and Cole showed him the beginning tree of William Green's land (being on the main Rolling Road leading from Baltimore Town into Britain Ridge forest about one-half mile from said town). John Cole showed deponent the boundary tree of where Charles Gorsuch then lived and he heard Gorsuch say his father John Cole showed him the boundary tree.

Deposition of William Green, 6 August 1750, age about 58: Some years ago he was with John Cole, Sr. on the west side of Mountenays Run and was shown the tree he bound as the beginning tree of "Cole's Addition."

Deposition of Thomas Gorsuch, 6 August 1750, age about 70: He said the place he now stands was called "Darley Path" and is on the main Rolling Road from Baltimore Town into Britain Forrest.

123. Petition of James Osborn, 1750: In reference to "Spry's Marsh." (pp. 198-201)

Commissioners appointed 10 August 1750: Thomas Franklin, William Smith, William Savory and Nicholas Ruxton Gay.

Deposition of Agnes Moore, 27 February 1750, age about 69: About 50 years ago she started to make crop with ---- Pritchard on his plantation on west side of Rumney Creek. She cut down a chestnut tree and John Chapman told it was a boundary tree. She also heard William Osborn the Elder and ---- Pritchard say it was a boundary tree of lands owned by William Savory and William Osborn, Sr.

Deposition of William Hollis, 27 February 1750, age about 54: About 16-17 years ago he was with William Osborn from over Rumney Creek on their way home from Mr. Mathews when Osborn showed him a tree stump on his land. Asked why he took up vacant land lately, he said that Mr. Phillips had bothered him and persuaded him to do it.

Deposition of Benjamin Osborn, 27 February 1750, age about 56: He identified the boundary tree that separated land of ---- Savory from his father William Osborn.

Deposition of George Chancey, 27 February 1750, age about 42: About 16 years ago, while with Joseph Pritchard, they saw the remains of a boundary tree which Pritchard said divided his lands from William Osborn's lands.

Deposition of William Hollis, 27 February 1750, age about 54: About 17-18 years ago he had heard William Osborn and Roger Mathews discussing "Spry's Marsh" and said it lay up Bush River near land called "Common Garden." Roger Mathews disagreed and said Oliver Spry had a survey made and it began at the lower marsh and ran up river. William Osborn, deceased, showed him beginning tree of "Common Garden."

Deposition of Jacob Hanson, 27 February 1750, age about 51: Says he heard William Osborn, deceased, identify the boundary tree of Osborn's land "Common Garden."

Deposition of Thomas Dennower, 27 February 1750, age about 45: Some years ago he saw the boundary tree at the landing place of William Osborn, deceased.

124. Petition of William Savory, 1750: In reference to "Cabbin Neck" on west side of Bush River. (pp. 202-204)

Commissioners appointed 8 March 1750: Nicholas Ruxton Gay, Nathan Richardson, James Maxwell and Thomas Franklin.

Deposition of George York, 30 March 1751, age about 70: About 50 years ago Capt. Thomas Preston showed him the beginning tree of "Cabbin Neck." About 30 years ago it was cut down by Mark Swift or someone in his family.

Deposition of John Thrift, 30 March 1751, age not stated: Said his father Richard Thrift and John Hopkins, late of Baltimore County deceased, carried chain for running out "Cabbin Neck" in Gunpowder Neck (between Gunpowder River and Bush River) and went by place where Abraham Taylor made clay and mud bricks, now called the "Brick Hole."

Deposition of Edward Mead, 30 March 1751, age about 72: About 30 years ago he was with Andrew Thomson who showed him the boundary.

Deposition of John Dawney, 30 March 1751, age about 60: About 26-27 years ago he was with Richard Thrift on path betwen the plantation where Thomas Brereton, deceased, lived and this place here, and Richard Thrift pointed out the line of "Cabbin Neck."

125. Petition of Jacob Giles, June, 1747: In reference to "Land of Promise." (pp. 205-212)

Sequence of events transpired as follows: In June, 1747, Giles filed his petition. On 6 August 1747, Court appointed Commissioners: Nicholas Ruxton Gay, Charles Worthington, Joseph Hopkins, and James Lee. On 17 August and 13 September 1747, Commission members qualified. On 15 October 1747, Commissioners took five depositions:

Deposition of Richard Perkins, age about 60: Before tract "Eightrap" was ran out, his father, Richard Perkins, told him about the beginning tree of Taylor's land "Friendship" and "Line's Tents." When Col. John Dorsey (the surveyor of Baltimore County) made resurvey of "Eightrap" he began 30 to 40 perches east and ever since that has been taken as the beginning tree of "Land of Promise," "Eightrap" and "Line's Tents."

Deposition of Isaac Webster (Quaker), age about 47: About 12-13 years ago at request of --- Derumple, stepfather to Benjamin Elk of Calvert County, the deponent requested commission to perpetuate boundary of "Friendship." Richard Perkins and Frances Foy gave evidence as to bounds on west side of Rock Run. Also note that Richard Perkins had died.

Deposition of Gregory Farmer, age about 67: About 20 or more years ago he was with Robert West and ran out line of "Line's Tents" to a little island at mouth of Deer Creek.

Deposition of Robert West, age about 79: About 40 years ago he knew of the boundary.

Deposition of William Perkins, age about 50: He understood that "Land of Promise" extended from the Susquehanna River to a red oak bound by Col. John Dorsey. About 20 years ago Daniel Collett settled on Taylor's land and tried to run the land. Some time later John Belcher and Daniel Collett took some land of Benjamin Tasker.

From 3 November to 24 November 1747, the Court received the reports of the Commission and George Rock's caveat. In March, 1748, George Rock again caveated. In June, 1748, George Rock appealed to Provincial Court. On 20 July 1748, the Commission took a 6th deposition:

Deposition of Frances Foy, age about 72: About 40 years ago she heard Richard Perkins, deceased, say that he was with Mr. Lightfoot when survey was made. She heard her deceased husband Daniel Johnson speak of the boundary and the bound tree of "Eightrap" was the bound tree for three tracts: Taylor's land, Harrison's land, and another she could not remember.

On 1 August 1748, George Rock filed a writ of certiorari via attorney Stephen Bordley, begging to transfer his case to the Provincial Court at Annapolis (filed bond dated 29 July 1748, although record says 1758). (No Date) George Rock of Cecil County caveats against the recording of depositions taken by Commission. Similar occurrence dated in March, 1747, and the Court ordered to not record. In June, 1748, the Court orders to record the depositions and George Rock asked to appeal to Provincial Court; it was granted. He filed a bond with Stephen Onion and William Dallam as securities for 4,000 lbs. of tobacco to pay Jacob Giles' costs if original findings by the Commission are affirmed, and to pay costs to Provincial Court.

Between 1748 and 1751 the Provincial Court acted and it appears they ruled in favor of Giles. On 24 May 1751, Giles filed writ of procedendo. In August 1751, Court ordered recording of all proceedings in this case.

Justices of Baltimore County Court, November, 1747: Thomas Sheredine, Parker Hall, William Bond, Thomas Franklin, Charles Ridgely, William Young, John Paca, Winston Smith, Edmond Smith and Samuel Owings.

126. Petition of Benjamin Mead, June, 1751: In reference to a 200 acre tract called "Francis Choice" on south side of Bird River. (pp. 213-217)

Commissioners appointed 3 August 1751: Walter Tolley, William Bond, Walter Dallas and Daniel Scott.

Deposition of Capt. William Bond (of Thomas), 18 September 1751, age about 44: About 7 years ago he was with Bazaleel Foster he went to resurvey land of Capt. Barnet Bond (now in possession of his brother, William Bond (of William). Bazaleel Foster showed him the beginning tree of his land "Winley's Forest" and of his father-in-law Benjamin Mead's land "Francis Choice."

Deposition of William Bond (of William), brother of Barnet Bond, deceased, now living on Barnet Bond's land, 18 Sept. 1751, age about 25: Four years ago he was with Bazaleel Foster who showed him the bounds. Deponent later came to live on his deceased brother's plantation on Bird River.

Deposition of Thomas Dulaney, 18 September 1751, age about 36: Some years ago Jos. Bevans said that about 36 years past the bounded tree was notched by Daniel McIntosh.

Deposition of Joseph Bevans, 18 September 1751, age about 70: About 36 years ago, walking from his then plantation to Winley's Creek (sometimes called Winley's Cove), he saw a recently notched tree and asked Daniel McIntosh, who laughed. McIntosh would not say he notched the tree, but claimed he got a warrant and took up a piece of land in Neville's Neck. Neighbors believe McIntosh cut the notches himself to make people believe he had taken up the land. Deponent doens't believe the tree is the bounded tree of any land.

Witnesses: Thomas Baillie and Jacob Starkey.

127. Petition of Anthony Asher, 1751: In reference to "Chadwell's Range," now called "Asher's Purchase" and lying on south side of Salt Peter Creek on Philip's Island. (pp. 218-219)

Commissioners appointed 4 November 1751: William Bond, Daniel Scott, Walter Dallas and Luke Raven.

Deposition of John League, 1 April 1752, age about 49: About 1750 Jacob Cross said he had taken up land on south side of Saltpeter Creek called "Jacob's Privilege" and his beginning tree was the second tree of "Chadwell's Range." About 18 years ago Bloyce Wright and his son Thomas showed him and identified a stump as the second bounded tree of "Chadwell's Range."

Deposition of John Jones, Sr. (Middle River Neck), 1 April 1752, age about 55: About 28 years ago Bloyce Wright told him the boundary.

128. Petition of Charles Carroll, Esq. & Company (Anne Arundel County), 1752: In reference to a tract called "Orange" and its boundary on "Long Point" on Herring Run. (pp. 220-223)

Commissioners appointed 8 August 1752: John Ridgely, Nicholas Ruxton Gay, William Lux and Charles Carnan.

Deposition of Philip Jones, 1752, age about 50: In 1731 he was deputy syrveyor in Baltimore County and made resurvey for Dr. Charles Carroll of "Old Georgia" near or including land of Baltimore Iron Works, adding vacant land which lay between two of Charles Ridgely's tracts where the dwelling of Lyle Goodwin now stands. One day he was at the house where Charles Wells formerly lived. Was with Dr. Carroll, and his brother; Mr. Charles Ridgely; and John Baltenbury.

Deposition of Thomas Broad, 14 November 1752, age about 60: About 46 years ago his father, John Broad, showed him the bounded red oak, the beginning tree of "Long Point," taken up by David Jones and then possessed by Richard Cromwell. John Broad said some time before, he and John Wilmot, Sr. and Jr., Richard Cromwell, and Thomas Beale were at the tree and Richard Cromwell asked John Wilmot, Jr. to rebound it, and John Wilmot, Sr. said he was person who first bound it when David Jones took it up. Deponent said he often heard his father, John Broad, deceased, and John Wilmott, Jr., deceased, speak of this.

129. Petition of George Pain (Anne Arundel County), 1752: In reference to tract "Fry's Plains" near Walter Tolley's dwelling plantation. (pp. 224-226)

Commissioners appointed 8 August 1752: Captain William Dallam, John Hammond Dorsey, William Bond & Walter Dallas.

Deposition of Major Thomas Franklin, 10 June 1753, age about 46: About 30 years ago he was riding from the Long Calm, a fording place of the great falls of the Gunpowder River, and near to the place where the Free School now stands, in company with Barbara Redman who showed him the beginning tree of David Frye's land near Walter Tolley's old field and near a small pond.

Deposition of Thomas Sligh, 10 June 1753, age about 50: About 6 years ago he was with Charles Crooke, deceased, and Heathcote Picket, who is now living, and they showed him the boundary.

Deposition of John Roberts (alias Campbell), 10 June 1753, age about 60: One of the bounded trees was also the bound tree of a tract called "Betty's Inheritance."

Deposition of James Lennox, 10 June 1753, age about 48: About 9 years ago Walter James, deceased, told him that some years before on way to Thomas Tolley, Sr. he saw Thomas Tolley, Jr. and John Gambrill (servant to Thomas Tolley, Sr.) bring down a bounded tree of tract called "Betty's Inheritance."

Deposition of Henry James, 10 June 1753, age about 30: His father, Walter James, told him of the boundary.

Note in record states Commission didn't set up boundary post because Walter Tolley wouldn't let them.

130. Petition of John Atkinson, 1752: In reference to "Parker's Choice." (pp. 227-228)

Commissioners appointed 29 May 1752: John Hall (Cranbury), James Osborn, Joseph Lusby and John Paca.

Deposition of William Hollis, 14 July 1752, age about 56: He was hunting about 37 years ago and set his gun down against a bounded tree as told to him by John Parker who owned the land "Parker's Choice." About 16-17 years ago deponent was with Joseph Yeats who showed him a bounded tree of "Collier's Meadow" and said he had seen the tree 15 years before that near --- Ananias' old field. William Osborn and John Parker showed him the boundary.

131. Petition of Renaldo Monk, March, 1753: In reference to "Cook's Adventure" bounded by "Turkey Cock Hall. (pp. 229-230)"

Commissioners appointed 10 March 1753: Samuel Owings, George Ashman, Cornelius Howard and Joseph Cromwell.

Deposition of James Chilcoate, 9 June 1753, age about 51. About 25 years ago he was with Richard Gist who told him of the beginning tree of "Turkey Cock Hall" and Gist said he sold an 80 acre part of the tract to Edward Riston.

Deposition of John Cook, 9 June 1753, age about 46: Said he made a survey of "Cook's Adventure" about 9 years ago, and he and Edward Riston swapped lands.

Deposition of Josephus Murray (Quaker), 9 June 1753, age about 64: Pearce Welch showed him the boundary.

Deposition of Samuel Hooker (Quaker), 9 June 1753, age about 67: About 42 years ago Dutton Lane told him the bounded tree belonged to "Turkey Cock Hall," to Carroll's land, and to Pearce Welch's land.

132. Petition of Robert Boone (Anne Arundel County), 1752: In reference to "Edward and Will's Valles and Hills." (pp. 230-232)

Commissioners appointed 30 November 1752: William Govane, Joseph Cromwell, John Willmott and Edward Stevenson.

ABSTRACTS OF BALTIMORE COUNTY LAND COMMISSIONS

Deposition of Samuel Merriman, Sr., 24 March 1753, age about 70: At a place on east side of Jones Falls was once a bounded tree. He carried chains when land was surveyed. Bounded tree was also bounded tree of "Merrimans Pasture."

Deposition of Samuel Meredith (planter), 24 March 1753, age about 40: About 17-18 years ago William Barney told him that the third tree of "Edward and Will's Valles and Hills" was the beginning tree of "Stevensons Enlargement" and he carried chain when Edward Stevenson, Sr. had his land run out in presence of Robert Boone and others.

133. Petition of Robert Collins, 1753: In reference to "Pork Hill," containing 100 acres in the forest on the drafts of Winter's Run, and whose bounds are not rightly settled. (pp. 233-234)

Commissioners appointed 10 March 1753: Roger Boyce, Benjamin Norris, Daniel Preston and James Preston.

Deposition of Jacob Bull, 21 April 1753, age about 67: About 25 years ago he was shown the bounds.

Deposition of John Bond, 21 April 1753, age about 40: About 20 odd years ago he was with his father and some others and was shown the bounds.

Deposition of John Roads, 28 April 1753, age 32: Within the past year he was at Thomas Bond, Sr.'s, and he told him the bounded tree of "Pork Hill" was boundary also of "Hewit's Range."

134. Report of William Smith, 14 September 1753: In reference to "Jonathan's Inheritance," a tract on Deer Creek, bought by his father, William Smith (miller) from Jonathan Jones, son of Jonathan Jones (carpenter), who originally took up the land. The beginning tree on east side of Deer Creek was accidently cut down and a stone was set up as the boundary, in the presence of William Bennett, John Skinner, James Lee, Henry Beach, John Dunn, Alexander Hill, and Edward Morgan. (pp. 235)

135. Petition of Andrew Rhodes on behalf of Nicholas Carew and Company, 1752: In reference to tract called "Grindon." (pp. 236-237)

Commissioners appointed 30 November 1752: Thomas Franklin, Nicholas Ruxton Gay, Bryan Philpot and William Lux.

Deposition of Thomas Broad, 28 December 1752, age about 60: About 17-18 years ago, Major Thomas Sheredine, John Ruston, Luke Stansbury, John Lee (all deceased), and Thomas Franklin (deputy surveyor) came to deponent's house and said they had warrant to run out new tract for the Kingsbury Company and asked deponent of the bounds.

Deposition of Thomas Franklin, 28 December 1752, age about 47: About 17-18 years ago he laid out 3000 acre "Grindon" (gave statement similar to Thomas Broad).

136. Petition of George Grover, 6 June 1753: In reference to 150 acre tract "Daniel's Town" and 50 acre tract "Waterton" on south side of the Gunpowder River. (pp. 238-239)

Commissioners appointed 9 June 1753: Walter Dallas, Isaac Raven, William Bond and George Harryman.

Deposition of Charles Pine, 20 August 1753, age about 47: When he was about 17 he was hired as servant of George Grover, deceased, grandfather of present George Grover, and he knows of the bounds on west side of the Gunpowder.

Deposition of Anthony Asher, 20 August 1753, age about 53: About 40 years ago George Grover I and George Grover II told him of the bounds, and the second tree of "Daniel's Town" was also the beginning tree of William Denton's "Denton's Hope." He was also told this by William Denton.

137. Petition of Thomas Johnson, 7 November 1753: In reference to "Turkey Cock Hall." (pp. 240-242)

Commissioners appointed 9 November 1753: John Ridgely, Nicholas Ruxton Gay, William Lyon and William Lux.

Deposition of James Welch, 13 May 1754, age about 42:About 20 years ago he met Samuel Hooker in the woods and he showed deponent the beginning tree of his father's land "Welches Adventure" and also a bounded tree of Mr. Carroll's "Turkey Cock Hall." He also had a resurvey of "Welches Adventure" about 2-3 years ago.

Deposition of James Gardner, 13 May 1754, age about 50: About 2-3 years ago he was surveying ffrom the beginning tree of John Cook's "Adventure" south to beginning tree of "Turkey Cock Hall" and James Welch said that Joseph Murray said the tree was the bounded tree of "Later Louns" ... near John Taylor's cleared ground.

Deposition of Renaldo Monk, 13 May 1754, age about 52: About 4 years ago John Cook told him the boundary, and about 2 years ago James Welsh told him the boundary.

Deposition of Edward Stevenson, 13 May 1754, no age given: About 20 years ago James Welch showed him the tree of his father's land and mentioned Pierce Welch. Samuel Merryman, Sr., about a fortnight or 3 weeks before his death, told bounds to deponent and Thomas Johnson and Benjamin Jervis.

Deposition of Benjamin Jervis, 13 May 1754, age about 23: About 2 months ago Samuel Merryman showed him the bounded tree of his land and said Asagel(?) Israel's plantation was within land Samuel Merryman formerly owned.

Deposition of Ambrose Gehoghagen, 13 May 1754, age about 25: About 3 years ago he carried chain when Edward Riston (deceased), who owned "Turkey Cock Hall," and John Cook ran out its bounds.

Deposition of Samuel Merryman, 13 May 1754, age about 32: Deponent's father, Samuel Merryman, told him of the bounds of the property.

138. Petition of John Cromwell (Anne Arundel County), 1752: In reference to "Maiden's Dairy," "Cromwell's Range," and "Cordwainer's Hall," being contiguous. (pp. 243-249)

Commissioners appointed 29 May 1752: Nicholas Ruxton Gay, Maberry Helms, John Ensor, Jr. and William Lux.

Deposition of Emanuel Teal, 13 November 1753, age about 40: About 8-9 years ago Charles Pierpont, Sr., deceased, told him the bounds. When he was a boy and even up to manhood the land was called "Hooker's Dairy," presumably after Hooker who took up the land.

Deposition of George Bailey, 13 November 1753, age about 80: About 40 years ago Isaac Larogue, formerly servant of Richard Cromwell, deceased, but then still living on Cromwell's land, showed him the bounds, north of the road from Richard Cromwell's quarter to Capt. Stinchcomb's.

Deposition of Charles Pierpont (son of Charles, deceased), (Quaker), 13 November 1753, age about 33: About 10 years ago his father pointed out a tree on Dead Run as boundary.

Deposition of George Bailey, 13 November 1753, age not given: About 45-46 years ago he was at Thomas Cromwell's plantation where Mahaleel Shittle(?) now dwells. Thomas Cromwell said his uncle, Richard Cromwell, told him about the boundary.

ABSTRACTS OF BALTIMORE COUNTY LAND COMMISSIONS

Deposition of Richard Marsh, 13 November 1753, age about 41: About 18 years ago he found his brother J... Marsh and John Feaster (a sawyer) cutting the tree.

Deposition of Richard Marsh, 20 February 1754, age about 41: About 8-9 years ago William Maclean showed him the bounded tree of William Cromwell and said he was running the land.

Deposition of Charles Hissey, 20 February 1754, age about 52: About 30 years ago James Jackson, overseer for Capt. John Cromwell, showed him the beginning tree of "Cordwainer's Hall" which was the upper tree of "Cromwell's Range." About 29 years ago James Yitcham told him which was the bounded tree of Hope's land and Cromwell's land.

139. Petition of William Cockey, 1753: In reference to "Cockey's Folly," "Cockey's Trust," "Helmore," and "Helmore's Addition" on north side of Jones Falls.

Commissioners appointed 9 November 1753: Cornelius Howard, Thomas Johnson, Thomas Bond and Edward Stevenson.

Deposition of Nathan Tipton, 30 June 1754, age about 105: About 40 years ago he was with Edward Stevenson, Dutton Lane and Pierce Welch at the beginning tree of "Cockey's Trust," the second tree of "Celsed," and the beginning tree of "Carsas Forrest." About 40 years ago he heard Edward Stevenson tell John Cockey that the third tree of "Cockey's Trust" was the beginning tree of Carpenter's land.

Deposition of James Chilcoat, 30 June 1754, age about 50: About 30 years ago Richard Gist told deponent and Jonathan Tipton that he lived near here about 20 years ago and John Cockey told him that Thomas Cromwell had told him of the bounds. He was also told the bounds by John Cockey, John Boreing, and Thomas Tipton.

Deposition of John Tipton, 30 June 1754, age about 52: About 34 years ago John Boreing told him the bounds. About 40 years ago John Cockey told him the bounds.

Deposition of Samuel Owings, 30 June 1754, age about 52: About 10-12 years ago John Cockey told him and William Cockey of the beginning trees of "Cockey's Folly" and "Cockey's Delight."

Deposition of Edward Tulley, 30 June 1754, age about 66: About 40 years ago he and Pierce Welch were on the road leading from Oulton's Garrison to John Cockey and Pierce Welch told him the bounds.

140. Petition of John Watkins, 1753: In reference to "Matthew's Chance" in Spesutie Hundred on Delph Creek. (p. 250)

Commissioners appointed 30 November 1753: James Steward, John Hall (Spesutie), James Garretson and James ---.

Deposition of John Clark, 7 August 1754, age about 69: About 1729-1730 he was employed by John Watkins, deceased, (father of petitioner) to run land, and Thomas Williamson and Thomas Birchfield told him the bounds. On 4 November 1731 John Watkins, deceased, hired him to lay out 30 acres of vacant land adjoining "Matthew's Chance." Some years later Aquila Paca, deceased, asked him to run dividing line between "Matthew's Chance" and the land Aquila Paca escheated, formerly belonging to Martin Depost.

141. Petition of John Frazier (ship carpenter), 5 June 1753: In reference to "Todd's Forrest," a 250 acre tract near Satyr's quarter. (pp. 251-252)

Commissioners appointed 9 June 1753: Samuel Owings, Thomas Gist, Cornelius Howard and John Gill.

41

Deposition of Abram Vohan, 13 October 1753, age about 63: About 30 years ago Richard Gist came to lay out the tract "Nicholson's Mannor" for --- Nicholson, and deponent carried chain.

Deposition of Josephus Murray (Quaker), 13 October 1753, age about 64: About 30 years ago he carried chain for Richard Gist to lay out "Nicholson's Mannor" and then to lay out land for Lawrence Todd.

142. Petition of John Day and Benjamin Ricketts, 1754: In reference to "Maxwell's Conclusion" near "Warrington." (pp. 253-254)

Commissioners appointed 6 December 1754: John Howard, Walter Tolley, Robert Adair and George Presbury.

Deposition of William Savory, 20 March 1755, age about 50: About 19 years ago John Baldwin and William Rumsey (Cecil County) had escheat warrant for "Warrington." Col. White (surveyor) and William Rumsey notched a walnut tree in presence of John Baldwin, Aquilla Mercey, William Hill, Thomas Dawney and Christopher Divers in place of a stump which old Benjamin Legoe showed them.

Deposition of Christopher Divers, 20 March 1755, age about 57: He gave a statement similar to William Savory.

Deposition of Thomas Ensor, 20 March 1755, age about 37. About 9-10 years ago Thomas Dawney told him the bounds.

Deposition of Benjamin Legoe, 20 March 1755, age about 38: About 3 years ago his father told him the bounds.

143. Petition of Thomas Ward, 1755: In reference to "Lusby's Adventure" and "Fawn's Forrest." (p. 255)

Commissioners appointed 7 June 1755: Nicholas Ruxton Gay, John Ridgley, William Rogers and William Lux.

Deposition of William Parrish, Sr.(Quaker) 21 August 1755, age about 75: He was standing at three bounded white oak trees standing in west corner of Richard Demmitt's cornfield. About 20-30 years ago he was here with John Parrish (deceased) and surveyor when they bound one or more of the trees for beginning of "Fawn's Forrest."

Deposition of Edward Stevenson, 5 September 1755, age about 52: About 27 years ago he was employed by Philip Jones, Jr. as deputy surveyor, and was called by John Parrish (deceased) to lay out land for Thomas Lusby. Came to level opposite head of branch descending into Gwin's Run and about one-half mile northwest of Richard Demmitt's plantation and ran bounds.

144. Petition of Amy (Amg?) Dawes of Calvert County, 1755: In reference to "Batson's Fellowship." (pp. 256-258)

Commissioners appointed 3 June 1755: John Paca, Sr., William Bradford, Aquila Hall and Jacob Lusby.

Deposition of Antil Deaver, 5 August 1755, age about 71: In September about 54 years ago, Edward Batson began to run out land for Bennett Creed in presence of Bennett Creed, William Derumple and John Derumple (all of Calvert County) and John Deaver (father of Antil), John Miles, and Stephen Freeland (all of Baltimore County), starting at a red oak in field formerly called "Miles' Old Field" but now called "Holland's Old Field." He came to live in Baltimore County in February and the above land was run out the following September, adjoining Creed's land, and east of plantation where Richard Deaver, Sr. formerly lived. "Chestnut Ridge" was where Daniel Judd formerly lived. John Derumple was whipt by first red oak mentioned.

ABSTRACTS OF BALTIMORE COUNTY LAND COMMISSIONS

Deposition of Thomas Tredway, 5 August 1755, age about 54: (Apparently he stated he knew something about the bounds of land, and his statement was similar to Deaver's above.)

Deposition of John Deaver, 5 August 1755, age about 40: About 20 years ago he knew that a red oak was the bounded tree of Holland's land, and when his father came in 1732 to take up "Addition to Stoney Ridge," this was his second tree. About 13-14 years ago Col.White told him the bounds.

Deposition of Lewis Puttee, 5 August 1755, age about 45: Last January he was carrying chain to run out land for Mr. Amg (Amy?) Daws. Deponent also mentioned "Batson."

Deposition of Col. Thomas White, 5 August 1755, age about 50. (Apparently he knew something about the bounds of the land and acknowledged the statement of John Deaver above.)

145. Petition of John Atkinson, 1753: In reference to "Parker's Choice." (pp. 259-260)

Commissioners appointed 30 November 1753: George Hollandsworth, John Mathews, John Hall (Cranbury) & James Steward.

Deposition of William Hill, 15 March 1754, age 50: Said that Benjamin Legoe, Sr. said that Richard Morton told him the beginning of "Abbey Island" was at the mouth of Abbey Island Creek.

Deposition of James Osborn, 15 March 1754, age 42: Father told him John Parker's tree...was in a cornfield next to Drews...and John Parker showed him. William Hollis was evidently before Commission in 1753 and said tree was of "Collins Meadow."

146. Petition of Nathan Bowen, 1755: In reference to "Samuel's Hope." (pp. 261-264)

Commissioners appointed 7 June 1755: William Govane, Nicholas Ruxton Gay, Christopher Carnan and John Ensor.

Deposition of Samuel Hooker (Quaker), 15 September 1755, age about 68: About 50-52 years ago he was with his father Thomas Hooker, deceased, who showed him the beginning tree of "Samuel's Hope," "Oulton's Fellowship," and "Lane's Triangles." About the same time, Dutton Lane, deceased, told him of the bounds. About 5-6 years later he was with old Nicholas Haile and Teague(?) Todd(?) and he saw Moses Edwards and William Barney carry chain for Major Richard Colegate, deceased, to run out "Oulton's Fellowship." His father said the surveyor was a rogue and bound the wrong tree and the mistake was found by James Murray who had the adjoining land. Deponent's father went to Charles Carroll, Esq., and reported it. About 52-52 years ago he was with his father on east side of Jones Falls and Rowlands Run and, near the main road from Benjamin and Nathan Bowen's over Rowlands Run, his father showed him the bounded tree of Thomas Hooker's land "Samuel's Hope" and also "Rector's Hopyard." Later, Dutton Lane, deceased (uncle of Samuel Hooker) told him of the bounds.

Deposition of Dutton Lane (Quaker), 15 September 1755, age about 53: About 40 years ago his father told him this was the beginning tree of affirmant's uncle Hooker's land and his (Dutton Lane, Sr.) land, i.e., "Samuel's Hope" and "Lane's Triangles." About 20 years ago deponent understands there was a dispute between William Barney and Morgan Murray over the bounds. About 25 years ago John Boreing, deceased, told him the bounds.

Deposition of Richard Hooker (Quaker), 15 September 1755, age about 54: About 40 years ago his father Thomas Hooker and William Wheeler had some dispute about bounds and got Dutton Lane, deceased, to run out the land.

Deposition of Edward Stevenson, 15 September 1755, age about 52: Last summer Benjamin Bowen and Samuel Hooker were at his house and Samuel Hooker told the above story. Last year he was brought here to Jacob Young to begin to run out Jabez Murray's part of "The Hopyard."

Deposition of Jabez Murray, 15 October 1755, age about 56: He understood the tree on west side of Jones Falls was the bounded tree of "Morgan's Delight" and "The Hopyard" which formerly belonged to him but now to heirs of George Bailey (deceased) and deponent was here with Richard Gist, George Buchanan (deceased), John Risteau, Edward Tully, Thomas Hooker (deceased), Samuel Hooker, and others, when tree was proved.

147. Petition of John Carnan and wife Achsah, 1755: In reference to "Huntington," "Wilkinson's Folly," "Edward's Lot," and part of "Edward's Enlargement." (pp. 265-268)

Commissioners appointed 6 December 1755: Brian Philpot, Nicholas Ruxton Gay, Nicholas Rogers and William Lux.

Deposition of John Edwards, 2 February 1756, age about 50: He heard John Merryman, deceased, say which was the beginning tree of "Merryman's Lot" and "Huntington." About 30 years ago his father Moses Edwards told him and showed him the bound. On the road from plantation where Moses Edwards lived to Baltimore was "Edward's Enlargement." And on the great road from Baltimore Town up to Brittain Ridge he was shown the tree bound under 3 years ago and claimed by John Ensor and son Joseph as bounded tree of "Darby Hall."

Deposition of Richard Rutter, 26 February 1756, age about 42: West of house where Thomas Rutter, deceased, formerly dwelt, his father Thomas Rutter told him of the bounds of "Edward's Enlargement."

Deposition of Joseph Ensor, 26 February 1756, age about 26: About 3-4 years ago, bounding "Darby Hall," his father John Ensor, owner of "Darby Hall," told him about the bounds.

Deposition of Thomas Gorsuch, 26 February 1756, age about 78: About 30 or more years ago John Ensor, deceased, showed him the bounds. Deponent's land called "Ensor's Choice" abutted "Darby Hall." East of the plantation of Elizabeth Price, Moses Edwards, deceased, often showed him the bounded tree of his land, but if the tree that John Edwards proved above is the bounded tree of "Huntington," it would take away some of deponent's land. Jonathan Hanson also told him it was Edwards' land.

148. Petition of Richard Ruff, 1755: In reference to "Daniel's Lott Revised," above the head of Bush River, adjoining "Ranger's Lodge." (pp. 269-270)

Commissioners appointed 3 June 1755: John Hall (Cranbury), Robert Adair, Aquila Hall and Jacob Lusby.

Deposition of Thomas Bond (Quaker), 27 October 1755, age about 77: About 48-49 years ago he served on Commission regarding "Ranger's Lodge" with Aquila Paca and William Howard and John Webster, and the bounds ran descending into James' Run. Negro John Elberton said his master, Thomas Thurston, then deceased, told him the bounds, but Col. Phillips who owned the land said the bounds were in sight of Eynum's Run.

Deposition of Antil Deaver, 27 October 1755, age about 71: Stephen Freeland and Thomas Thurston showed him the land bounds, and Thomas Thurston said his father had his negro John Elberton cut it down because it was the bounded tree of Col. Phillips' land. Also mentioned the bounded tree of "Thornbury" which Thomas Thurston offered to sell.

Deposition of Thomas Tredway, 27 October 1755, age 54: He was the chain carrier to run out "Ranger's Lodge" for Mrs. Martha Paca, and was with Benjamin Jones, John McComas, John Webster, and either Samuel or John Deaver. Also named John Crockett and property near Antil Deaver's plantation.

149. Petition of Cornelius Howard, 9 August 1754: In reference to "Lun's Lott." (pp. 271-273)

Commissioners appointed 10 August 1754: Thomas Franklin, Samuel Owings, Joshua Owings and Bryan Philpott.

Deposition of Philip Jones, 27 September 1754, age about 53: About 1726-1727 he was surveying "Lun's Lott" within two perches of the west side of Jones Falls (draft of the northwest branch of Patapsco River) and about 50 yards below where Jonathan Hanson is now building a stone mill house on east side of the falls.

Deposition of William Parish (Quaker), 27 September 1754, age about 74: About 40 years ago he was with Moses Edwards (late of Baltimore County, deceased) who showed him the beginning tree of Eager's land called "Lun's Lott."

Deposition of William Parish (Quaker), 28 September 1754, age about 74: Not far from dwelling house of William Lux, formerly dwelling house of Dr. George Walker, on the south side of great road from Baltimore Town, some years ago he was with Richard Gist (late of Baltimore County, deceased) who told him the bounds.

Deposition of Philip Jones, 28 September 1754, age about 53: He knew of the land on east side of Gill's Branch and the bounded tree of "Lun's Lott."

Deposition of William Parish (Quaker), 28 September 1754: Moses Edward said the bounds were on the east side of the main road from Baltimore Town to Patapsco River, and he knew of the bounded tree of Charles Ridgely's land called "Timber Neck."

Deposition of Philip Jones, 28 September 1754: He knew of the bounds by the northwest branch of Patapsco River and close to beginning of Baltimore Town. Richard Gist (late of Baltimore County, deceased) showed him the bounds.

(Note: No reason was given but this case wasn't written up and sent to Court until 5 February 1757.)

190. Petition of Samuel McCarty, 1758: In reference to "Jackson's Hazard," adjoining "Timber Proof" between Musketoe and Delph Creeks. (pp. 274-277)

Commissioners appointed 12 May 1758: Amos Garrett, Joseph Lusby, David Bissett and George Lester.

Deposition of James Garrettson, 5 February 1759, age 49: He saw the bounds that were run by John Hall of Swan Town.

Deposition of William Daugherty, 5 February 1759, age about 51: Some years ago John Jackson said there was vacant land in Redbird Neck. When he and John Jackson were going from Martin's Landing on Delph Creek down the creek in a canoe, John Jackson showed him the tree of Stokes' land.

Deposition of John Mathews, 5 February 1759, age about 43: Apparently knew of the bounds, but no details were given.

Deposition of John Hall (Cranbury), 1 March 1759, age not given: He and Capt. Aquila Paca knew of the bounds on Delph or Martin's Creek.

Deposition of Thomas Donavin, 1 March 1759, age not given: Mentioned a church as bounds, and Reddyon (Redlyon) Bridge which George Stokes said was a boundary of his and Paca's land, now Richard Garretson's.

151. Petition of Col. William Young on behalf of Rebecca Stokes widow, executrix and orphan of Robert Stokes, deceased, late of Baltimore County, 1757: In reference to "Harmar's Town" lying on the Susquehanna Ferry. (pp. 278-282)

Commissioners appointed 3 December 1757: John Mathews, William Husbands, Amos Garrett and William Dallam.

Commission met 2 November 1759, but then learned that adjoining land, on which the resurvey of "Harmar's Town" may depend, called "The Convenience," was owned by Philip Darnall of Anne Arundel County, and the law requires that proprietors of lands adjoining those on which Commission is granted be notified. Col. Young produced Thomas Lucas, age about 27, who swore that on 3 September 1759 he posted advertisement at door of Parish where Rev. Lake is rector, and where Philip Darnall resides in Anne Arundel County.

Deposition of William Hollis, 2 November 1759, age about 63: About 1719 a ferryman told him the tree belonged to Stokes' land. Also mentioned a spring used by Mary Deaver.

Deposition of Ford Barns, 2 November 1759, age about 35: About 20 years ago he was with Richard Deaver who showed him the bounds.

Deposition of John Deaver (of Richard), 2 November 1759, age about 44: He was with Talbot Risteau (Ristean) at the first point ("Point Conquest") made at the mouth of the Susquehanna River, adjoining land called Stokes' land, or "The Ferry Land," or "Harmar's Town."

Deposition of James Allen, 2 November 1759, age about 50: About 17 years ago Humphrey Wells Stokes told him about the bounds, and later with Talbot Risteau (Ristean) and Daniel Preston he had some involvement in "Harmar's Town."

Deposition of Daniel Preston, 12 November 1759, age about 44: About 4 years ago Robert Stokes told him about land.

152. Petition of William Woodward of Annapolis, 1759: In reference to "The Land of Goshen." (pp. 283-287)

Commissioners appointed 12 November 1759: John Carnan, Nicholas Ruxton Gay and Samuel Owings.

Deposition of Emanuel Teal, 31 March 1760, age about 46: About 30 years ago William Baker, who then lived in the Patapsco forest, showed him the land taken up by John Israel.

Deposition of Henry Owings, 31 March 1760, age not given: About 4-5 years ago Nicholas Baker and Emanuel Teal showed him the land.

153. Petition of Aquila Carr and Thomas Cole, Jr., 1760: In reference to "Price's Goodwill." (pp. 288-291)

Commissioners appointed 10 March 1760: John Colegate, Samuel Worthington, John Merryman and Nicholas Merryman.

Deposition of Benjamin Wheeler (Quaker), 22 May 1769, age about 34: About 11 years ago Mordecai Price (who took up the land) showed him bounds on south side of Western Run.

Deposition of Mordecai Price, 22 May 1760, age about 26: (Quaker, and son of Mordecai Price who took up the land) About 11 years ago his father showed him the bounds, and he carried chain to lay off part of the land which his father was exchanging with Aquila Carr because Aquila Carr had built his house on said land.

Deposition of Abraham Cole, 22 May 1760, age about 34: About 8 years ago he and Mordecai Price and Aquila Carr ran out the land.

Deposition of John Hooker, 22 May 1760, age about 35: About 13-14 years ago Aquila Carr told him the bounds.

154. Petition of Skipwith Coale, 5 March 1760: In reference to "Phillip's Purchase" on west side of the Susquehanna River. (pp. 292-295)
   Commissioners appointed 10 March 1760: Ephraim Andrews, Corbin Lee, Edward Hall and Edward Morgan.
   Deposition of Richard Wells, 5 May 1760, age 66: About 30 years ago he showed Colonel Nathan Rigbie the way to John Hawkins, deceased, who knew the bounds.
   Deposition of Joseph Lee, 5 May 1760, age 55: About 16 years ago he saw William Rumsey, deceased, run out bounds of "Phillip's Purchase."

155. Petition of Abraham Jarrett, 1760: In reference to part of "The Deserted Lott" leased to Abraham Jarrett, deceased, on or near Stirrup Run. (pp. 296-298)
   Commissioners appointed 9 June 1760: Capt. William Smith, James Scott, Edmund Talbott and Mordecai Amoss.
   Deposition of John Bond (Quaker), 28 July 1760, age about 48: Abraham Jarrett asked him to survey "The Deserted Lott" (in his "Lordship's Reserve") adjoining "Bond's Last Shift." Also mentioned were James Billingsley and William Crafton.

156. Petition of George Ensor, 1760: In reference to "Spring Garden." (pp. 299-303)
   Commissioners appointed 10 March 1760: William Rogers, Benjamin Wheeler, William Dowland (Noland), & Joshua Hall.
   Deposition of Dennis Garrett Cole, 22 May 1760, age 54: About 20 years ago Edward Richards (who originally took up the land) sent his son Benjamin to show deponent the bound trees below the ford of Western Run (on the north side of Western Run within 5 yards and about 20 perches from east side of main road from dwelling house to Baltimore Town). His brother, John Cole, later bought "Spring Garden" and later sold it to Capt. Henry Morgan who told his overseer, John Emmitt, the bounds.

157. Petition of John Ensor, Sr., 1757: In reference to "Darby Hall." (pp. 304-308)
   Commissioners appointed 5 March 1757: William Rogers, Nicholas Ruxton Gay, Brian Philpott and William Lux.
   Deposition of Richard Rutter, recorded 6 August 1760, age about 44: About 20 years ago his father, Thomas Rutter, told him of the bounds.
   Deposition of Thomas Corsuch, Sr., recorded 6 August 1760, age about 77: When Jonathan Hanson (deceased) surveyed his own land, deponent was shown the bounds.
   Deposition of Charles Green, recorded 6 August 1760, age about 61: About 40 or more years ago Moses Edwards showed him the dividing tree between him and John Ensor's land.
   Deposition of John Edwards, recorded 6 August 1760, age about 53: About 30 or more years ago his father, Moses Edwards, showed him the bounds.

158. Petition of William Andrews, 1760: In reference to "Salt Petre Neck" in Middle River Neck. (pp. 309-312)
   Commissioners appointed 9 June 1760: Thomas Franklin, Walter Tolley, John Skinner and William Young.
   Deposition of John Denton, 23 July 1760, age about 42: About 15 years ago his father, William Denton, told him of the bounds.

Deposition of James Dollarhide, 23 July 1760, age about 41: About 28 years ago his father-in-law, William Denton, late deceased, told him of the bounds.

159. Petition of Richard Garrettson, 1760: In reference to "Dispatch" on drafts of Delph Creek. (pp. 314-319)
Commissioners appointed 9 June 1760: Joseph Lusby, James Osborn, Luke Griffith and Greenberry Dorsey.
Deposition of John Jackson, 23 July 1760, age 47: About 19 years ago his father, John Jackson, showed him the bounds.
Deposition of Edward Garrettson, 23 July 1760, age about 33: About 7 or more years ago John Jackson, Sr. told him the bounds.
Deposition of James Garrettson, 23 July 1760, age about 50: About 11 years ago John Jackson, Sr. told him the bounds.
Deposition of John Jackson, 23 July 1760, age about 47; The tree claimed by Mr. Stokes' heirs and Mr. Paca is not the bounded tree of any person, but it was bound by Hugh Brannican as a frolick. Deponent's father showed him the bounds of Stokes' land.
Deposition of Edward Garrettson, 23 July 1760, age about 33: John Jackson, Sr. told him something similar to what John Jackson said above about the bounded tree.
Deposition of John Garrettson, 23 July 1760, age about 54: He was with Edward Garrettson and John Jackson, Sr. and was told same as above statement.

160. Petition of Robert Scott, 1760: In reference to "Moorfields." (pp. 320-324)
Commissioners appointed 10 November 1760: John Howard, Thomas Lingan, James Gittings and Walter Tolley.
Deposition of Maurice Baker, 20 May 1761, age about 59: About 8-9 years ago he carried chain to run out "William's Ridge" for Nathan Horner and the bounded tree was about 20 yards from the southwest side of Gunpowder Neck Road that leads to the head of Bush River.
Deposition of Lemuel Baker, 20 May 1761, age about 49: About 27-28 years ago he knew the bounds when he carried chain to run out Robert Scott's land.
Deposition of Endimion Baker, 20 May 1761, age about 46: He carried chain to run out land of Robert Scott, and his father Charles Baker told him the bounds and that he lived near this tree about 50 years ago. And John Armstrong, who is now here, also told him the bounds.
Deposition of Samuel Smith (of Gunpowder Lower Hundred), 20 May 1761, age about 55: About 24-25 years ago Lawrence Fouracres (who lived near above tree) said it was the tree of Robert Scott and ---- Phillips.

161. Petition of Henry Wetherall, 1760: In reference to "John's Interest" (by resurvey of "Linnen Manufactury"). (pp. 325-328)
Commissioners appointed 10 November 1760: John Howard, Thomas Lingan, James Gittings and Walter Tolley.
Deposition of John Fulton, 29 June 1761, age about 40:About 8-9 years ago Henry Wetherall employed him, and Jonathan Hughs showed him the bounds.
Deposition of William Bradford, 29 June 1761, age about 25: About 8-9 years ago he was chain carrier when Jonathan Hughs showed him the bounds.
Deposition of Daniel McComas (of John), 29 June 1761, age about 30: Gave same statement as William Bradford above.
Deposition of James Board, 29 June 1761, age about 52: He was with Daniel McComas and William Bradford when Jonathan Hughs showed them the bounds.

162. Petition of Thomas Ford, 1761: In reference to "Selsed" ("Selsead") near Jones Falls. (pp. 329-336)

Commissioners appointed 8 June 1761: Joseph Cromwell, George Risteau, Cornelius Howard and John Bond (of Chesnut Ridge).

Deposition of Samuel Hooker (Quaker), 23 November 1761, age about 75: About 50 years ago his father showed him the bounds and about 25 years John Boring also knew them.

Deposition of Dutton Lane (Quaker), 23 November 1761, age about 61: About 30 years ago Samuel Hooker, Richard Hooker and John Boring were talking about "Selsead" and John Boring said there should be a bounded tree right behind Thomas Carr's fence.

Deposition of Thomas Tipton, 5 December 1761, age about 67: He had a land warrant located near "Selsead" and had surveyor John Clark run bounds of "Selsead" to discover vacant land, and he came to beginning trees of Thomas Carr's land.

Deposition of James Richards, 14 December 1761, age about 40: In 1747 Capt. Henry Morgan told him that John Merryman had told him that Thomas Carr had his negroes cut down the tree and grub out roots, but the Hookers knew the bounds.

Deposition of James Chilcoat, 14 December 1761, age about 62: About 30 years ago John Clark was surveying to discover surplus land for Jonathan Tipton, but Henry Satyr told Tipton not to execute the warrant there as it would be detrimental to Anne Plowman.

Deposition of Richard Hooker (Quaker), 10 February 1762, age about 62: About 30 years ago he and Samuel Hooker and Dutton Lane and John Boring were talking about the bounds.

Deposition of Absalom Barney, 10 February 1762, age about 59: About 6-7 years ago he and William Welsh were talking and Welsh said Carr's land bounded "Selsead." Welsh died better than 1 year ago; never heard father say anything.

Deposition of Mary Rutter, 10 February 1762, age about 61: When she and husband William Barney were riding from the plantation of Thomas Carr (deceased) to Charles Robeson's (deceased) he showed her and told her of the bounded tree.

163. Petition of Charles Ridgely, Alexander Lawson and Benjamin Bowing (Bowen) by attorney Thomas Johnson, Jr., 1762: They requested not to record the above Commission record of Thomas Ford on grounds that (1) Cornelius Howard is related to Thomas Ford; (2) They took Richard Hooker's deposition on 23 November 1761, but destroyed it, and took a second deposition later which differed materially from the first, but even then omitted a material part of the second deposition; (3) Petitioners have had not chance to examine witnesses; (4) Petitioners made requests, oral and written, for a chance to produce their own witnesses, but were ignored; and, (5) Several tracts of land owned by the petitioners may be swallowed up in "Selsed." (pp. 336-337)

On 4 June 1762 the Commissioners rejected this petition, and ordered it to be recorded.

164. Petition of William Andrew, 1762: In reference to "Middle Jenifer" in Middle River Neck. (pp. 337-340)

Commissioners appointed 5 June 1762: William Young, Walter Tolley, John Skinner and Thomas Sligh.

Deposition of John Parks, 13 October 1762, age about 40: About 23-24 years ago Abraham Enlowed showed him the bound tree of Selman's land near his own, about 80-90 yards from the present dwelling house of Anthony Enlowes.

Deposition of William Jerman, 13 October 1762, age about 44: About 20 years ago Anthony Enlowes showed him bounds.

Deposition of William Jones, Jr., 13 October 1762, age about 40: William Gracer (?) told him the bound tree was destroyed by a boy about 14-15 years old by the name of Charles Maxwell.

165. Certified, 31 May 1762: The bound tree of Thomas Lucas' condemned land has been cut down by accident and replaced with other bound trees and a stone. Signed by following: Ranroe (X) Richison, Isaac (X) Wright, William Bradford, and Henry Bennett Darnall.

166. Petition of James Kimble, 1762: In reference to "Parkinton" on branches of Musketto Creek. (pp. 341-347)

Commissioners appointed 5 June 1762: Amos Garrett, James Stewart, Richard Garrison and Michael Gilbert.

Deposition of Thomas Cord, 1762, age 58: Rowland Kimble, deceased, told him the tree belonged to "Parkinton" and "The Grove."

Deposition of James Taylor, 1762, age 50: About 18 years ago Richard Kimble had Amos Garrett (deputy surveyor) run bounds of "Expectation" and he began at beginning tree of "The Grove."

Deposition of Dan Johnson, 1762, age 50: About 16 years ago John Clark said this tree is the beginning tree of Dr. Middlemore's tract called "The Grove."

Deposition of Samuel Kimble, 1762, age 37: His father, Richard Kimble, told him the bounds, and since father's death, brothers William and James Kimble know the bounds.

Deposition of Thomas Everest, 1762, age 36: About 12 years ago he came here at request of Colonel John Hall, and John Clark (dec'd.) showed him the bound tree of "Beaver Neck."

Deposition of John Clark, 1762, age 22: He was with Thomas Everest and remembers a small dispute between his father, John Clark, and Colonel John Hall.

Deposition of Dan Johnson, 1762, age 50: About 5 months ago he was here with James Kimble, John Clark and Colonel John Hall in reference to the bounds of "Beaver Neck."

Deposition of Samuel Kimble, 1762, age 37: About 5 months ago an agreement was made between James Kimble and Colonel Hall regarding the bounds of "Beaver Neck" and "Maschal's Humour."

167. Petition of Benjamin Rogers, 1762: In reference to "Parker's Haven" and "Kemp's Addition." (pp. 348-354)

Commissioners appointed 14 August 1762: John Ridgely, Nicholas Ruxton Gay, William Lux and Brian Philpott.

Deposition of William Green, 18 October 1762, [age not legible]: About 40 years ago he helped Major Colegate survey Nicholas Rogers' land at mouth of Norris Creek (now Harris' Creek).

Deposition of Thomas Gorsuch, Sr., 25 October 1762, age about 81: About 50 years he was at house of Thomas Hedge and heard Thomas Hedge point out Rogers' tree to John Ensor (deceased).

51

54

MACCOMAS, Daniel 48, 116
 William 48
MACLEAN, William 138
MACNEMARRA, Michael 110
MAHAM, Edward 24
MAHONE, John 120
Maiden's Dairy 138
Margrett's Delight 25
MARSH, J. 138
 John 2
 Richard 138
MARSHALL, Mary 6
MARTAIN, John 103
MARTAINE, John 79
Martaineson 41
MARTIN, Laowdeweck (Ludowick) 23
 Lodwick 64
Martin's Creek 150
Martin's Landing 150
Martin's Neck 41
Martin's Rest 31
Mary's Bank 60
Mary's Plains 84
Mascall's Hope 2
Maschal's Humour 166
MASON, Robert 52
 Thomas 52
MASSEY, Aquilla 60
 Jonathan 60
Mate's Angle 63
MATHEWS, Elizabeth 118
 Henry 30
 James 14
 John 92, 106, 113, 115, 145, 150,
  151
 Mr. 123
 Roger 12, 17, 40, 48, 49, 58, 59,
  63, 64, 78, 118, 123
Matson's Lott 116
Matthew's Chance 140
MAXWELL, Charles 164
 Col. 15
 James 19, 30, 60, 73, 80, 124
Maxwell's Conclusion 142
MC CARTY, Samuel 150
MC COMAS, Daniel 161
 John 148
MC CUBBIN, William 103
MC INTOSH, Daniel 126
MEAD, Benjamin 126
 Edward 124
MERCEY, Aquilla 142
MEREDITH, Samuel 132
Merrikan's Inheritance 99
MERRIMAN, Samuel 28, 132

Merrimans Pasture 132
MERRYMAN, Capt. 112
 Charles 112
 John 97, 112, 147, 153, 162
 Joseph 112
 Mary 112
 Nicholas 153
 Samuel 112, 137
Merryman's Lot 147
Middle Jenifer 164
Middle River Neck 158, 164
MIDDLEMORE, Dr. 57, 166
 Josias 21, 57
MILES, John 144
Miles' Old Field 144
MILHUSE, Bart. 87
Mill Branch 63
MILLAM, Henry 59
MILLAN, Henry 58
MILLER, Henry 66
MILLHUSE, Bartholomew 18
MITCHELL, Thomas 26, 31, 52, 54, 113
MOALE, John 39
MONK, Renaldo 131, 137
Monntenay's Run 47
MOORE, Agnes 123
 Edward 49
 James 105, 115
 Nicholas Ruxton 94
Moorfields 160
MORGAN, Edward 134, 154
 George 52, 54, 113
 Henry 104, 114, 156, 162
Morgan's Delight 28, 114, 146
MORRIS, -- 64
 Thomas 23, 26
MORROW, James 83
Mother's Care 78
Mount Organ 121
Mountain, The 112
Mountanys Run 122
Mountenays 86
Mt. Savall 63
MURDAUGH, Daniel 119
MURPHY, Patrick 4
MURRAY, George 93
 Jabez 28, 114, 146
 James 28, 39, 53, 146
 Joseph 114, 137
 Josephias 28
 Josephus 51, 85, 104, 114, 117, 131,
  141
 Morgan 28, 114, 146
Muskeeto Creek 23
Musketo Proof 66

ROGERS, Nicholas 147, 167
  William 39, 47, 65, 84, 91, 122,
    143, 156, 157
ROLLO, Archibald 1, 11, 115
Rork Run 56
Rowlands Run 146
ROWLES, Jacob 41, 50
ROYSTON, John 95
RUARK, Patrick 9
RUFF, Daniel 106, 115
  Richard 81, 148
Rumley Creek 57
Rumney Creek 123
RUMSEY, William 33, 142, 154
RUSTON, John 135
RUTLEDGE, Michael 18
RUTTER, James 93
  Mary 162
  Richard 147, 157
  Thomas 147, 157
Salt Peter Creek 18, 87, 127
Salte Petre Neck 158
SAMPSON, -- 40
  Isaac 22, 42, 95
Sampson's Thickett 60
Samuel's Delight 62
Samuel's Hills 46
Samuel's Hope 146
SATYR, -- 141
  Henry 162
SAVAGE, Elinor 39
  Hill 39
SAVORY, -- 123
  William 99, 100, 123, 124, 142
Sawpit Point 120
SCOTT, Daniel 11, 15, 18, 21, 45, 48,
    81, 90, 118, 126, 127
  James 155
  John 18
  Robert 160
Scott's Lott 48
Seader Run 96
Sedgely 21
SEELEY, Emanuel 26
Segley 15
SELMAN, -- 164
Selsed 163
Selsed (Selsead) 162
Seneca Ridge 16
SERGANT, John 112
Setter Hill Run 108
SEWELL, Major 107
Sewell's Fancy 94, 107
SHARD, Thomas 118
SHEPPARD, Nathaniel 16

SHEREDINE, Thomas 3, 4, 8, 32, 36,
    37, 42, 50, 55, 68, 71, 72, 86, 89,
    94, 95, 97, 98, 102, 107, 112, 122,
    125, 135
SHIE, Thomas 45
SHITTLE, Mahaleel 138
Shoemaker's Hall 71
SICKLEMORE, Samuel 11
Sicklemore's Dock 11
SIMMONS, Charles 107
  Isaac 67
SIMPSON, Richard 31, 42
  Thomas 31
  William 31, 63
SING, John 112
SINKINS, John 121
SKINNER, John 134, 158, 164
SLIGH, Thomas 95, 129, 164
SMITH, Charles 1, 10, 72, 75, 83
  Edmond 125
  Edward 5
  Elizabeth 57, 112
  John 94
  Mary 5
  Nathaniel 115
  Richard 10
  Samuel 112, 160
  Walter 10
  William 5, 15, 19, 21, 29, 59, 93,
    115, 123, 134, 155
  Winston 125
  Winstone 113
  Zachariah 30
Smith Range 46
SMITHEN, James 98
SMITHERS, -- 109
  James 63, 77, 83, 98
  Richard 49
SNOW, John 39
SOLLERS, Sabret 91
  Sabrit 103, 112
South Hampton 118
SPARROW, Solomon 7
Sparrow's Nest 7
Sparrow's Point 7
Spring Branch 48
Spring Garden 156
Spring Neck 77
Spring Point 4
SPRY, Oliver 123
Spry's Marsh 123
STANSBURY, Luke 1, 8, 10, 14, 27, 36,
    41, 68, 71, 72, 76, 78, 120, 135
  Thomas 37, 120
  Tobias 7, 32, 41, 95, 103, 108, 112

64